Critical Guides to French Te

Critical Guides to French Texts

EDITED BY ROGER LITTLE, †WOLFGANG VAN EMDEN, DAVID WILLIAMS

VERCORS

Le Silence de la mer

Frances M. Edge

Tutor in French
Woodhouse College, London

London
Grant & Cutler Ltd 2004

ISBN 0 7293 0435 3

DEPÓSITO LEGAL: V: 2.762- 2004

Printed in Spain by
Artes Gráficas Soler, S.L., Valencia
for GRANT & CUTLER LTD
55–57 GREAT MARLBOROUGH STREET, LONDON W1F 7AY

For Mike, Kate and Ju with my love and thanks

'Matériellement, physiquement, la France pouvait avoir succombé; qu'importait, tant que demeurait vive l'âme française' (*Les Editions de Minuit: historique et bibliographie,* Jaques Debû-Bridel, Les Editions de Minuit, 1945)

Contents

Contents

Prefatory Note

Vercors died on 10th June, 1991; I am grateful to him for his kindness, information and perceptive criticism, and to Mme Bruller-Vercors (the translator, Rita Barisse) for her help and interest. I also thank colleagues and friends, especially Dr Graham Townsend, for help and advice, my editor, Professor Roger Little, for his patient and expert guidance and Mr. Raymond Howard for all his help. My thanks also go to the Senior Managers of Woodhouse College for leave of absence and to the Principal and Fellows of St Hugh's College, Oxford for their hospitality. Finally, I thank my husband and daughters for their encouragement, and my husband particularly for informed comment and computer expertise. The edition used is *Le Silence de la mer et autres récits* (Livre de Poche, 1993); this study is concerned only with *Le Silence de la mer*, although I refer to some of the other *récits* as part of the historical and literary background

Italicised numbers, followed where appropriate by a page reference, refer to the numbered items in the Select Bibliography at the end of this volume.

Enfield, May 2003   F.M.E.

Introduction

Despite an initial print run of only 350 copies, produced and distributed under extremely difficult conditions, *Le Silence de la mer* provoked extraordinary interest on its first publication. Such was the enthusiasm that numerous home-made copies were eagerly produced and distributed, and rumours abounded as to which well-known author was masquerading as 'Vercors'. It has been translated into seventy-two languages, made into a film (by Jean-Pierre Melville in 1948), adapted for the stage (first performed in Paris in 1949) and remains a very popular set text. Because it was conceived both as a work of commitment and as a work of literature, it cannot be fully appreciated without considering relevant aspects of the history of the period and of the author's life and opinions.

Although Vercors' literary output included fiction, biography, translation, memoirs and history, he tends to be remembered only for *Le Silence de la mer*. In an interview in *Le Figaro Littéraire,* "Vercors: 'Je ne suis pas l'homme d'un seul livre' *(17)* he reveals his exasperation at being largely ignored in literary circles and by the media since the post-war era, perhaps because he was self-effacing and unwilling to compromise his integrity by courting popularity, both in his private life and in his writings.

Jean Bruller, born in 1902, never intended to become a writer. After gaining his *brevet d'ingénieur* to please his father, he disliked so much his brief experience of engineering as a career that he went off to the studio of René Ménard to develop his flair for drawing and painting. Although he was a gifted painter *(13*, pp.45–48) — Picasso once found it difficult to distinguish his original painting from copies Bruller had made of it *(13*, p.153), he decided to make his living through drawing and engraving. After military service, he became a commercial artist for an advertising firm, but felt that he was on a treadmill. He had been amusing himself by producing sardonic sketches, and published an album depicting a variety of possible methods of committing suicide, entitled *21 recettes pratiques de mort violente*. This was important for several reasons: the captions underlining the black humour of the drawings were a transition between art and writing, he gained publishing experience, and he met Pierre de Lescure, with whom he founded Les Editions de Minuit, where that experience proved valuable.

Bruller met Lescure in 1926 when he walked into Lescure's religious bookshop looking for subscriptions to *21 recettes de mort violente*. Impressed, Lescure invited Bruller to submit sketches to accompany a series of talks given by literary personalities, then to write reviews of luxury editions of art books for the journal *La Quinzaine critique des livres et des revues* until the shop closed in 1932.

The success of *21 recettes...* led to Bruller being in great demand as an illustrator; his output including illustrations of works by Maurois, Kipling, Chamson, Aveline, Racine, Shakespeare and Poe. He also continued with albums of drawings, all, like *21 recettes...*, exhibiting world-weary nihilism and cynical humour. He was an absurdist before Sartre and Camus, with mockery as his only reason for bothering to produce anything. However, the care he took over the appearance of his work presaged the importance of elegance in the editions of *Le Silence de la mer*.

Between the wars, Bruller was a 'pacifiste à tous crins', strongly influenced by his future brother-in-law, Pierre Fort, whose account of the slaughter of Verdun convinced him of the horrifying reality and futile nature of war. In politics, Bruller was and remained a left-wing sympathiser without ever joining a political party, always referring to himself as a 'compagnon de route' of the Communists (*9*, p.214) An admirer of Aristide Briand, he pinned his hopes on reconciliation between France and Germany until it became obvious that war was inevitable.

Much of the background information about *Le Silence de la mer* and *Les Editions de Minuit* comes from Vercors's own accounts. In *Pour Prendre Congé* (1957), Vercors's withdrawal from public life, he expresses bitterness at various perceived injustices (*9*, p.20) including being forced out of Les Editions de Minuit by Jérôme Lindon in 1954 and being vilified in print by Lescure for having claimed a share with Lescure in the founding of Les Editions de Minuit (see Coda: The Post-War History of Les Editions de Minuit).

With *La Bataille du silence*, ten years on, written in response to requests for a written record of the circumstances surrounding the writing of *Le Silence de la mer* and the founding of Les Editions de Minuit (*10*, p.11), this mixture of self-justifying anger and self-pity (in the repeated image of a cracked pot left on a shelf) is replaced sometimes by overt but more often by tacit self-justification. What therefore amounts to a hidden agenda explains two irritating features of *La Bataille du silence*: that of a seeming prescience of major events of the war, to raise his self-esteem and to give added credence to his version of events, and of Pangloss-like recitals of causes and their effects which had led him to write *Le Silence de la mer* and so to found Les Editions de Minuit. His self-justification sometimes involves some re-writing of the past, and William Kidd lists instances of this (*45*, pp.43–49), but because of the scrupulous honesty and black and white view of morality which he exercised all his life, and which were often the cause of trouble (see Coda: The Post-War History of Les Editions de Minuit as well as numerous instances in *9*, *13* and *81*), I do not believe that he consciously lied. Rather, as his main motive was to clear his name, he saw the truth only from his own point of view, thus laying himself open to charges of deliberate selective memory.

The tale of how he, not Lescure, coined the name 'Les Editions de Minuit' (*10*, p.202), is to defend it as his, not Lescure's brainchild and also to stress all that it owed him despite Lindon's rejection of him. The list of all the influences and ideas behind *Le Silence de la mer* (*10*, pp.182–85), culminating in his communicating them to Lescure (*10*, p.193), also presented a way of responding to a novel by Lescure in 1959 (*La Saison des consciences*) which cast doubt on Vercors's authorship of the text. One of the characters, Conscience, could easily be seen as a mocking portrayal of Vercors's tender conscience (*81*, pp.31–36). It seems likely that this was in response to *Pour Prendre Congé,* published just two years earlier, as much of this deals with Vercors renouncing public office on grounds of conscience. Vercors's self-vindication in *La Bataille du silence* tends to be repeated in *Les Occasions perdues* and in *Les Nouveaux jours*, and even in 1991, in conversation with Gilles Plazy (*A dire vrai*), he felt his name still blackened by Lescure's attacks (*13*, p.116).

Lescure left no memoirs and could not respond to *La Bataille du silence*, written after his death. In her detailed study of Les Editions de Minuit (*81*), Anne Simonin seeks, through hitherto unknown archive material, to redress the one-sided account given by Vercors in his autobiographical writings. In this volume I discuss her main findings, which, together with an awareness of Vercors's self-justificatory agenda, particularly in *La Bataille du silence*, are necessary for as balanced an assessment as possible of *Le Silence de la mer* and its context.

1. The Context of Publication

From Pacifism to Resistance

The inevitability of war was brought home to Bruller, when, at the invitation of Jules Romains, he travelled across Germany to Prague to his first meeting of the PEN club, seeing for himself the extent to which Nazi values had supplanted those of the old culture. The cold, cruel eyes of an official, the crude anti-semitism ('Interdit aux chiens et aux Juifs' on a restaurant door even in old Nuremberg), the new fortifications of the Siegfried Line, all filled him with foreboding. The warm welcome by the Czechs, who looked to the French for support against Hitler, made him feel frustrated and angry with the French government for its inertia. On the literary front, Vercors saw his membership of the PEN club as 'mon premier pas dans le royaume des lettres' (*10*, p.28).

Bruller's despair at the lack of will to oppose Hitler, both in France and Great Britain, led to a change of attitude, with nihilism giving way to a desire to fight Nazism: 'Après Munich, il n'a plus été question de pacifisme, tant j'étais convaincu qu'il ne restait de choix qu'entre la guerre et la servitude' (*13*, p.75).

Real war involved a humiliating defeat of unimaginable speed, the German tanks smashing through the Ardennes forest, skirting round the Maginot Line and taking the ill-equipped and bemused troops completely by surprise. With the evacuation of Dunkirk and the second German offensive on 5 June 1940, hordes of panic-stricken civilians took to the roads in the 'exode', harrassed by the Luftwaffe, and not knowing why they were leaving their homes or where they were going.

After a brief skirmish with the enemy, Bruller's battalion was stationed in Peyrus, at the foot of the Vercors *massif*, and it was there that the gaze of a local girl reminded him of Stéphanie, a former girlfriend. He tried to exorcise feelings of guilt that he had allowed the relationship to die by fictionalising the romance: 'c'était aussi mes premières armes comme écrivain' (*10*, p.104). The revival of these feelings also gave the idea for the love between the niece and the officer in *Le Silence de la mer*.

He spent the rest of the summer in what had now become known as the Zone Sud, as France had been partitioned under the terms of the Armistice on 22 June into the occupied north and unoccupied south. The latter was now governed by the eighty-four year-old Maréchal de France and hero of the Battle of Verdun, Philippe Pétain, based in the little spa town of Vichy, ideally placed near the border between the two zones and a secluded hotbed of intrigue. Pétain's broadcast of 16 June, made before shaking hands with Hitler at Montoire and signing the humiliating Armistice, contained the defeatist phrase 'il faut cesser le combat', provoking Vercors's outburst: 'Mais les uns comme les autres, quand la voix chevrotante de Pétain, à la radio de midi, annonça qu'il fallait "cesser le combat", nous restâmes accablés. Tout au fond de nous-mêmes, jusqu'à cet instant-là, nous avions…espéré un miracle… '(*10*, pp.75–76).

He felt shame and disgust at the attitude of his compatriots, who, taking their lead from Pétain, welcomed their conquerors with open arms. It was soon business as usual in Paris, with shopkeepers eagerly selling to the Germans luxury goods which the French could not afford. Posters depicting caring, smiling German soldiers appeared, and were borne out in reality. The occupying forces seemed to pose no threat; they were courteous, helpful, scrupulous in paying for their needs, gave smiling greetings… — it was hard to believe the rumours of their brutality in the invasion of Czecho-slovakia and Poland. Vichy propaganda strengthened this feeling by playing on the need for a sense of security after the shock of invasion and defeat, portraying Pétain as a venerable grandfather figure who knew that it was best for France to get on well with the Germans, to forget about fighting for freedom, and instead to live up to the new slogan: 'Travail, Famille, Patrie' (*78*, p.10). By 1941, many industrial and commercial enterprises were pursuing a policy of cooperation with Germany to safeguard their profits and to lay foundations for future prosperity should Germany win the war (*69*, pp.185–89). Vercors reflects this policy of the Germans to bribe and flatter the French in von Ebrennac's warning that it is the soul of France, its national identity, which the Germans want to overcome: '«…Pourquoi supposez-vous que nous avons fait la guerre? Pour leur vieux Maréchal?»…«nous avons l'occasion de détruire la France, elle le sera…Son âme surtout…Nous la pourrirons par nos sourires et nos ménagements…»' (p.53). In other words, they will not be satisfied with the surrender at Montoire, contrary to Pétain's opinion (*69*, p.173). [1]

A note from the mayor of his village of Villiers-sur-Morin, Brie, told Bruller that he would need to return at once to reclaim his home in which some German soldiers had been billeted. Surprisingly, the Brullers found that not only had there been no damage, but it was obvious that great care had been taken to prevent anything from being spoiled. A problem concerning the officer who came to greet them focused Bruller's attention on what was to become the main theme of *Le Silence de la mer*: how should one respond to a good man who is the tool of an evil ideology? The officer was no stereotype of a Nazi stormtrooper, but had 'un gentil regard dans un visage rebondi d'aspect plutôt latin, fendu d'un large sourire' (*10*, p.115), and whose courteous remarks about the house would normally call forth a friendly response. However, nauseated by the fawning that he had witnessed during the first months of Occupation, Bruller was instinctively frosty, and weeks later in the street refused the officer's greeting, then immediately felt remorse. The next time they met, it was in the presence of someone else whose fury at the French defeat was, if anything, even greater than Bruller's. Obviously, this made it impossible for Bruller to greet the German, and it also occurred to him that a greeting at this stage would, in any

---

[1] William Kidd states that the 'Maréchal' is presumably Foch (*49*, p.21), but Mme Bruller/Vercors replied to my query on this: 'You are quite right, of course, that 'leur vieux Maréchal' refers to Pétain and not to Mal. Foch!' (*87*)

case, have been tantamount to an apology for previous rudeness (*10*, p.115).

This dilemma, and Bruller's solution to it, gave the idea for the relationship of the uncle and niece with the German officer in *Le Silence de la mer*: a pattern of behaviour is instinctively established between them from the moment of the officer's arrival: 'D'un accord tacite, nous avions décidé, ma nièce et moi, de ne rien changer de notre vie, fût-ce le moindre détail, comme si l'officier n'existait pas; comme s'il eût été un fantôme' (p. 25). The niece's tenacity is based on the impossibility, as Bruller found, of altering his behaviour, while the uncle's doubts ('je ne puis sans souffrir offenser un homme, fût-il mon ennemi' (p.25, and see *10*, p.147), and 'C'est peut-être inhumain de lui refuser l'obole d'un seul mot' (p.29) echo those of Bruller himself at these awkward moments.

This real-life episode also shows Bruller's development from an ardent supporter of reconciliation with Germany and support for Briand to implacable opposition (*13*, p.75). The three characters of *Le Silence de la mer* illustrate this shift: von Ebrennac represents the Briand side until disillusioned; the uncle holds a middle position, afraid that his silence will cause offence, while the niece opposes the enemy despite her feelings for von Ebrennac. We see the extent of the niece's sacrifice, which readers are intended to note and emulate, while the uncle and von Ebrennac develop towards the niece's position, as Bruller did: the uncle by continuing to maintain his silence and von Ebrennac by violently rejecting his Briandist views, enhancing the message that the niece's stance is the only way to save France.

In August 1940 Bruller had briefly made contact with Pierre de Lescure, who now invited him to participate in resistance to the Germans through a network linked to the British Intelligence Service, the 'réseau Le Guyon' (*81*, pp.58–59) — Bruller was to help smuggle abroad British agents and crashed airmen. Although the network was soon put into abeyance through fear of infiltration, Bruller found the insistence on strict security in the Intelligence Service valuable experience for the strategies which would be needed in operating the clandestine Editions de Minuit. Lescure applied the rules to the letter: no names were ever to be written down, the only ones known were one up and one down the chain of command, so that contact could be made in each direction, and these names had to be memorised. Because of the risk of giving names under torture, the fewer people who knew anything, the better — so Bruller's wife and mother were unaware of his clandestine activities and of the identity of 'Vercors' until after the war. Vercors himself was very proud that no losses were suffered in all the hazardous work involved for Les Editions de Minuit (*10*, pp.11–12).

That autumn, a list of censored works had appeared, nick-named the 'liste Otto' after the German ambassador to Paris, Otto Abetz. Among the books banned were works by French, British, and above all, Jewish writers. The preface explained: 'Désireux de contribuer à la création d'une atmosphère plus saine, les éditeurs français ont décidé de retirer de la vente les livres qui ont systématiquement empoisonné notre opinion publique; sont visées en particulier les publications de réfugiés politiques et d'écrivains juifs qui, trahissant l'hospitalité que la France leur avait accordée, ont sans scrupule poussé à une guerre dont ils espéraient tirer profit pour leurs buts egoists…' Every French publisher, except for Emile Paul, had collaborated in the compilation of this list by suggesting authors whom they felt would offend the Germans. Some co-operated because, under the terms of the agreement, they avoided the delays involved in preliminary censorship, while others actively colla-borated out of sympathy with Nazi ideology; the overriding concern for all was to prevent the closure of their businesses. Bruller reasoned that to have anything published now would be tantamount to accepting these disgraceful terms, but it was difficult for many writers to see things in such black and white terms. They would lose their livelihood if they ceased to write or if their publishers were forced to close down or be taken over by Germans, who would be very selective in what they chose to publish. There was also the feeling that even if one allowed one's work to be cut by the German censor, at least French literature was being allowed to continue (*10*, pp.160–63).

The re-vamped *Nouvelle Revue Française* illustrates the kind of pressure being exerted. Gaston Gallimard, whose publishing firm was closed down for a brief period by the Propaganda-Abteilung, realised that he had to come to an agreement with the Germans to be allowed to re-open. Among the conditions was that the pro-Fascist Drieu la Rochelle was appointed editor of the *NRF* in place of Jean Paulhan, a widely respected literary figure; writers were invited to contribute under the pretence that nothing had changed. Bruller saw that the Germans had created an insidious way of infiltrating French minds; although people would be on their guard against overtly fascist periodicals like *Je suis partout, Gringoire* and *La Gerbe,* they would take the Nazi-infiltrated *NRF* at face value because of its integrity under Paulhan's editorship (*10*, pp.153–54).

The first example of clandestine publishing which Bruller came across was the newspaper *Pantagruel,* probably the first printed resistance newspaper (*61*, pp.32–37). Amazed and delighted, Bruller particularly admired two elements which were to be important to him in the publication of *Le Silence de la mer*: the elegant format and the measured tones of the editorial (*10*, p.156).

Bruller's priority was to make it clear that Nazism sought to control its victims mentally as well as physically, hence the distinction in *Le Silence de la mer* between 'dominer' and 'conquérir', and von Ebrennac's anguish at the end over the soul of France. This preoccupation was the hallmark of the intellectual Resistance, illustrated by Jacques Debû-Bridel, who helped in the distribution of *Le Silence de la mer*: 'C'était à l'esprit même de la France que l'ennemi victorieux s'attaquait' (*67*, p.10), and by Jacques Decour, pseudonym of Daniel Decourdemanche, one of the early martyrs of the Resistance: 'mais le plan hitlérien d'assassinat de la France est aussi un plan d'assassinat de l'intelligence française' (*Manifeste de front national des écrivains,* published posthumously in *Les Lettres françaises*, September 1942.

The turning point for Bruller to be able to put his ideas into practice came in February 1941, when with great ceremony and secrecy Lescure handed him a copy of a much more substantial publication than *Pantagruel,* entitled *La Pensée libre,* created by

Jacques Decour and others; Lescure most probably obtained his copy through his Communist connections (*81*, pp.72–73). In terms of clandestine publishing, it was an enormous step forward, but Bruller pointed out that it as it was Communist-inspired, it ran the risk of reinforcing German propaganda that only Jews and Communists were involved in resistance. Lescure agreed; the editors, in fact, had foreseen this problem, and had suggested that Lescure, with his wide literary contacts, should seek out new contributors from a broad range of anti-German opinion, even those from the far right who nevertheless supported a free France. After Bruller had visited Georges Duhamel, who refused to be involved as he had in the past had dealings with Communists, and wanted nothing more to do with them, he realised that other authors might well react in the same way, and Lescure pointed out that it was perhaps unwise to advertise their connection with a clandestine publication too widely. The solution, he suggested, was for the two of them to write the articles for the second issue themselves. He had approved of the drafts of the novel about Stéphanie which Bruller had continued with as intellectual stimulus to contrast with his day job as a carpenter's assistant and suggested he write a short story as well as articles for the next issue (*10*, pp.163–66).

As far as the articles were concerned, Bruller found topical subject matter easily enough, but ideas would not come for a story. To take his mind off the problem, and to earn more money, he turned to another project, this time an artistic one. He had decided to publish nothing while the country was under occupation, and certainly had not felt like continuing with humorous drawings, while his nihilist philosophy of life had been replaced by commitment to resistance. Nevertheless, he thought that he might try a very limited illustrated edition of *Silences* by Edgar Allen Poe, which would appeal to book collectors. The amount of detail he gives tacitly responds to Lescure's claim that it was he alone who had created both *Le Silence de la mer* and Les Editions de Minuit (see Introduction and The Post-War History of Les Editions de Minuit.

In the summer of 1941, a friend who was proof-reading *Silences* recounted a conversation between two German officers,

overheard by someone else, and which gave Bruller the inspiration he
needed for a short story. One officer in the overheard conversation
could not understand why German soldiers were behaving much
more kindly in France than in Poland, from which he had just
returned. His companion told him not to worry, as it was only a ruse
to lull the French to sleep, when they would be at the mercy of the
Germans. He ended by quoting in heavily accented French a sinister
line from Racine's *Britannicus*, where Nero shows his scorn for his
half-brother Britannicus's gullibility — the arms which embrace
Britannicus will soon strangle him: 'Ch'emprasse mon rival mais
c'est pour l'étouffer!' (*10*, p.182).

Bruller decided that the story would culminate in this
deception, and would feature a German officer who would not be like
those in the restaurant, but be based on the German Ernst Jünger,
author of *Jardins et routes,* an affectionate tribute to the beauties of
France and her culture, which Bruller had been re-reading. He
concluded that as Jünger was a German officer, he represented Nazi
ideology, of which he was either unaware or else he was writing a
clever piece of propaganda: 'Si Jünger n'était pas complice, il était
dupe' (*10*, p.181). The officer in *Le Silence de la mer* would himself
be a dupe of German propaganda, sincerely desiring the union of
France and Germany, symbolised by his desire to marry a
Frenchwoman. She, however, despite her attraction to him, would
resist his advances, and would not respond to his friendly
conversation. Finally, the officer himself would realise the Nazis's
real plans for France, and through his own horror at what he had just
learned, would powerfully convey to French readers the true nature
of the threat hanging over them. To the end, though, he would find it
impossible to disobey a régime whose ideology he now detested,
seeking death in action on the Eastern Front as the only possible
solution to his disillusionment.

Stéphanie, on whom the young woman is based, together with
the courteous officer who had been using Bruller's house, and whose
attempts at civility Bruller had ignored, provided two other elements
of the story. Bruller also recalled a francophile former German
officer he had met some years before on a ski-ing holiday, then again

just before the war in Paris, fleeing Nazism, ashamed and disgusted at his own people. The intriguing title, *Le Silence de la mer*, came after much searching and was inspired by Bruller's fascination with the sea and its suitability as a metaphorical representation of the Occupation; this is more fully discussed in *Facets of the Text*: The Sea.

The story was completed by the end of the summer of 1941, and was submitted to Lescure for approval. He read it right through in Bruller's presence, and, despite his normal impassivity, declared his approval at the end with tears in his eyes: 'De longtemps je n'avais plus ressenti une pareille émotion' (*10*, p.187). Fortunately, Bruller decided to hang on to the manuscript in case of any last minute changes, because within days *La Pensée libre* had been raided due to a traitor, the printer was in prison, and the editors had destroyed all remaining manuscripts before they fled. They immediately set about founding another review, *Les Lettres françaises*, but as this was to be much slimmer than *La Pensée libre*, so that fewer people would be involved, thus minimising the risk of betrayal, as there would not be room in it for *Le Silence de la mer*.

From this predicament came Bruller's idea of founding his own clandestine publishing house. As mentioned in the *Introduc-tion*, Vercors makes it clear at this point in *La Bataille du silence* that this was his idea, not Lescure's. He recalls that he had already published some of his albums himself, so why not publish this book, and if this one, why not others, by other writers? Clandestine publishing had so far consisted of ephemeral protest sheets, magazines and newspapers, but Bruller's venture would offer to authors who refused to publish the chance to earn a living, and, by so doing, show to the rest of the world that despite Nazi oppression, French culture was being kept alive. '...ne serait-ce pas pour l'étranger la preuve de la survivance sous la botte nazie de la vie spirituelle française? La preuve qu'elle tenait allumée dans la nuit, comme les moines de jadis, le flambeau dont la flamme se transmettrait de main en main...Une preuve qu'aucune feuille, aucun écrit de propagande, avec leur violence de ton...ne pouvait en fournir...' (*10*, p.189). Vercors goes on to say that Lescure was enthusiastic about the idea and wanted to help. The carefully worded conclusion to the second part of *La Bataille du silence*, marking the completion of *Le Silence de la mer* and the founding of Les Editions de Minuit, is further evidence of tacit self-justification, this time of why Bruller deliberately turned his back on armed resistance, unlike Lescure, whose experiences of this later coloured his attitude to Vercors (see Coda: The Post-War History of Les Editions de Minuit): 'Oui, au coeur de la Résistance française en train de naître dans la douleur, j'avais trouvé ma place et ma vocation: non dans l'action, dans ses violences et parfois ses erreurs; mais dans la sauvegarde, la persistence et l'exactitude de la pensée...' (*10*, p.189).

Les Editions de Minuit

The project was rapidly organised. It was decided that Lescure would take responsibility for literary matters, and that Bruller, with his numerous contacts in the world of printing and typography, would look after production and distribution. As far as security was concerned, they would succeed where *La Pensée libre* had failed, by applying the strict rules of security of the Intelligence Service, which, as Bruller already knew, were much tighter than those used by French resistance networks.

In November 1941, therefore, with the ostensible purpose of discussing his projected limited edition of Poe, Bruller went to see the printer Ernest Aulard, who had worked on many of his books, and with whom he shared an excellent relationship. Nevertheless, such were the dangers of denunciation for resistance sympathies, that Bruller did not come straight to the point. When he eventually came out with his proposition, Aulard said that of course he would help. Bruller explained that even though it was to be a clandestine publication, the book was to be produced on good quality paper with elegant typography. This in itself would be an act of defiance, showing to the outside world that not only could literature still be produced in France, but that under the extreme difficulties of the Occupation, such standards could still be maintained. Unfortunately, however, despite Aulard's enthusiasm, it was felt that his staff of over fifty people presented a security risk, but within a week, he had found the ideal person, Claude Oudeville[2], who printed wedding invitations and funeral notices on a tiny machine. As Oudeville's machine, with its small bed, could print only eight pages at a time, three months would be required, and that was thanks to Aulard lending him a typesetting machine. Aulard supplied type and was also able to supply paper, despite the rationing in force to prevent clandestine printing (*81*, p.91). All printing firms were allowed 10% extra to their requirements to allow for errors, but Aulard was such a careful printer that he never needed his (*81*, p.134). The binding and storage, beyond the scope of Oudeville's one-man business, would be undertaken by Yvonne Paraf, a friend of Bruller's from student days. Even she never knew until the end of the war that Bruller was Vercors, but a word she knew that Bruller always mis-spelled made her suspect it for a moment: 'déguingandé' for 'dégingandé' (p.19). Bruller quickly said that he had altered Vercors' spelling because he thought his own version was correct, and was amazed that she believed him (*10*, pp.210–11).

With some glee, Bruller had assumed in his dealings with Oudeville the name of the collaborating editor of the *NRF* Drieu (la Rochelle). He obviously needed a further pseudonym as author of *Le Silence de la mer,* and thought of how impressed he had been, when, from a troop train, he had seen the rugged grandeur of the Vercors (*10*, p.201). He eventually thought of an equally evocative name for the publishing house: Les Editions de Minuit, echoing the titles of Duhamel's *Confession de minuit* and Mac Orlan's *La Tradition de minuit*; this rather tedious account of the coining of the name (*10*, pp.201–02) is again to show that it all originated with him, not with Lescure.

Lescure had meanwhile managed to secure a promise of support from Paulhan who, because of his unsurpassed influence in the French literary world, was to play a major part in the development of Les Editions de Minuit. Lescure had been communicating with Paulhan through a member of his Intelligence Service network

---

[2] Recalled by Vercors as 'Georges' in *La Bataille du silence*, but attested elsewhere as 'Claude', notably in a list of Editions de Minuit shareholders (*81*, p.246).

who was codenamed "Lebourg", and who was Jacques Debû-Bridel,
an author with Gallimard and an employee at the Ministère de la
Marine, who had been passing information to Lescure about the
movements of the French fleet in the Mediterranean. Lescure also
contributed a preface which was inserted in all the volumes of Les
Editions de Minuit. As we have seen, Vercors and Lescure were of
one mind over intellectual resistance, and Lescure's preface echoed
Vercors' intentions above (*10*, p.289): to give authors the
opportunity to write freely and to eschew propaganda, thus
preserving the basic human right to read and write the truth: 'Voilà le
but des Editions de Minuit. La propagande n'est pas notre domaine.
Nous entendons préserver notre vie intérieure et servir librement
notre art…Il s'agit de la pureté spirituelle de l'homme' (*10*, pp.211–
12).

        Printing progressed steadily during December and January,
with Vercors paying weekly visits to Oudeville's shop to correct the
proofs and cycling off with the previous week's printed sheets, and
by 20 February 1942 all 350 copies of *Le Silence de la mer* were
ready, handsewn and bound by Yvonne Paraf and a small team of
trusted helpers. Vercors never took the sheets directly to Yvonne's
flat, but deposited them in an intermediate safe place, form where
they were collected by Pierre Massé, who was to become one of the
architects, under de Gaulle, of the Five Year Plan. The value of such
rigorous security, together with the assumed identities, was
highlighted by the arrest at that very moment of Jacques Decour, the
editor of *La Pensée libre* and *Les Lettres françaises*, and the
executions of Boris Vildé, Anatole Lewitsky and others. By sheer
chance, Les Editions de Minuit avoided disaster. Agents had been
selected to distribute the completed copies of *Le Silence de la mer*,
and to hand them over in the entrance hall of the Musée de l'Homme,
where there was always a great deal of coming and going. However,
a measure of the lack of cohesive resistance activity at this time is
that, unknown to Vercors, it was precisely in this building that one of
the earliest resistance networks had been formed. It had been
infiltrated and destroyed by the Germans; the recent arrests and
executions were of members of this *réseau*. It was obvious that the

Musée de l'Homme would be under strict surveillance, and before somewhere else could be found, Lescure put the whole operation on hold because of the arrest of one of the radio operators in his network, by whom he had passed information to London about the impending publication of *Le Silence de la mer*.

The postponement, which Vercors originally thought would be a matter of days, extended to months, then Lescure disappeared to the *maquis* to rejoin the réseau Le Guyon, leaving no means of contact. Not only therefore was *Le Silence de la mer* affected, but future projects of Les Editions de Minuit were jeopardised, since Debû-Bridel, the link with Paulhan, was of course unknown to Vercors except by his code name, Lebourg. Not wanting to break the security rules by contacting Paulhan directly, Vercors turned in desperation to Claude Bellanger, whom he knew to be a resistance contact of Lescure's (he was head of the group 'Maintenir'). Vercors used yet another pseudonym, 'Desvignes', which was to become his alias when dealing with the literary affairs of the Editions de Minuit, while he remained 'Drieu' for all contacts relating to the production side.

To Vercors's amazement, Bellanger revealed that not only had he and all his resistance colleagues already read the still unpublished *Silence de la mer*[3], but that numerous duplicated, typewritten and even hand-written copies were circulating from the one copy which Lescure had sent to Paulhan via Debû-Bridel. Paulhan had passed it on to the well-known paediatrician and resistance worker Professor Robert Debré, who had begun the process of duplication. Bellanger was effusive in his praise about the unknown Vercors, and this was the first instance of pleasurable irony which he was to feel because of remaining anonymous, and hearing a succession of famous writers identified as the certain author of *Le Silence de la mer*. Jacques Debû-Bridel, whose identity Bellanger had revealed to Vercors, told him that Gide and Roger Martin du Gard were contenders, while he himself favoured either Schlumberger or Arland. Vercors also

---

[3] In an unpublished memoir, Jean Lescure (no relation of Pierre) enthused about the text and stressed the positive effect of its elegant appearance (*81*, p.92)

learned from Debû-Bridel that Debré had contributed 5000 francs, which would go towards the cost of the next volume to be published.

This second title was to be *A travers le désastre* by the philosopher Jacques Maritain. Although Lescure had been aware of it before his departure, it was not yet in his possession. Vercors discovered that an edition of it had now appeared in the Zone Sud, published by Paul Hartmann, whom he already knew as a publisher of some of his albums. By false pretences he obtained an *Ausweis* to enable him to cross the frontier to see Hartmann, and also to try to organise some sort of distribution system for *Le Silence de la mer* in the Unoccupied Zone. His journey, undertaken in early July, was, however, only partially successful. Although he had obtained a copy of the Maritain text, he returned without it, as he had unwisely lent it to a friend, who failed to return it before Vercors's train left. He had, nevertheless, made contact with Suzanne Paraf, Yvonne's sister, who agreed to receive copies of *Le Silence de la mer*, while Yves Farge undertook their distribution.

Yvonne later managed to acquire a copy of *A travers le désastre* in the Zone Sud, and it was printed in the autumn. As Maritain was safely in America, his real name could be used, thus giving status to Les Editions de Minuit, and enabling him to write a preface echoing the prevailing theme of the intellectual resistance, that of opposing the Nazis trying to crush the spirit of France. The printing was much faster this time, because whereas Oudeville had had to reset the type for each run of eight pages, the recent recruitment of Maurice Roulois, a linotype operator working from home on a much larger machine, meant that the printing time was reduced from three months to two weeks.

With Roulois, Oudeville, and Yvonne's team of stitchers and binders, the production side was now operating smoothly. Distribution and the dearth of new material, however, continued to be a headache, partly because of Lescure's continuing absence. However a chance meeting with Jacques Lecompte-Boinet[4] ('Mathieu', head of the Resistance group 'Ceux de la Résistance'), led to a deal being

---

[4] Plaques to him and to Vercors were unveiled at the Left Bank end of the Pont des Arts on 25th February, 1992.

struck: men to transport type, proofs and copies in return for printing services (*42*, III, pp.18–19). Only a hundred copies of *Le Silence de la mer* had eventually been made available to selected recipients chosen by Bellanger and Paulhan, the rest being sent to the Zone Sud. Bellanger had told Vercors that this restricted distribution was causing something of a scandal in Parisian intellectual and resistance circles, and insisted that a second printing be undertaken. Yvonne, quite rightly, as it turned out, wondered if the delay in distribution now meant that the book was no longer relevant to readers in the Occupied Zone, because of increased repression and the massive round-up of Jews in the Vélodrome d'Hiver in Paris on July 16,1942. Though unconvinced, Vercors was nevertheless increasingly worried by the prolonged indecision (*10*, p.256).

He was also desperate for texts for Les Editions de Minuit; according to Jacques Debû-Bridel: 'Desvignes est obsédé par la crainte de ne jamais recevoir d'autres manuscrits' (*66*, p.51). In the winter of 1942–43 he decided to publish a collection of articles and poems, *Chroniques interdites*, with Paulhan, Yvonne Paraf, Debû-Bridel, Ponge, Benda and Vercors himself as the contributors. These contributions were in memory of writers who had suffered at the hands of the Nazis, so reflecting the increasing brutality of the Occupation. The tone, nevertheless, was restrained, as befitted Les Editions de Minuit, and as Vercors made clear in his preface: 'Ce n'est donc pas de la violence que l'on trouvera ici. Mais diverses tentatives, par divers hommes, d'atteindre à un fonctionnement serein de leur pensée, entre les murs de leur chambre, comme si ne tonnaient pas alentour les clameurs de la barbarie et de la mort.' This third volume marked an improvement in the scale and speed of the production process, because Aulard, with a machine capable of printing thirty-two pages at a time, was willing to take the risk, with only two trusted helpers, of printing at his works on a Sunday behind closed curtains and cleaning up meticulously afterwards. Today's computerised commercial printing processes bear little resemblance to 'real' printing (literally making an impression), and an awareness of the difficulties caused by noisy machinery, cumbersome setting up of metal type and removing all the evidence, emphasises the risks

involved. The publicity material for Jean Périmony's 1995
production of *Le Silence de la mer* pays tribute to this by featuring
Robert Doisneau's photograph of one of Oudeville's copies of the
text resting on a compositor's compartmentalised box of type
(reproduced in *79*, p.172).[5]

Distribution was always a problem, however, both to the
Unoccupied Zone and within Paris; Vercors recounts that the only
time he felt sheer terror during the Occupation was while passing the
same German sentry six times on his bicycle which was heavily laden
with batches of *A travers le désastre* (*10*, p.249). Vercors's initiative
in producing *Chroniques interdites* and in the rather makeshift
distribution of *Le Silence de la mer* were not, however, appreciated
by Lescure, who at last emerged briefly from hiding in February
1943, and insisted on taking sole charge of literary matters. Anne
Simonin says that as Bruller knew Lescure's address, he could have
contacted him, but was enjoying his independence (*81*, p.104).
However,this seems unlikely, because he had contacted Mme
Lescure over the delay in publication of *Le Silence de la mer*, only to
be told that her husband was *incommunicado*; this led to his
desperation and so to his subsequent meeting with Bellanger as the
only way of continuing (*10*, pp.219–20). Anne Simonin also says that
Bruller sought to avoid contact with Lescure as he was likely to be
angry that, having forbidden the distribution of *Le Silence de la mer*,
Vercors's disobedience in going ahead had led to the loss of two
hundred copies in a suitcase jettisoned by one of Lecompte-Boinet's
men. However, as Vercors mentions the loss specifically only in *Les
Nouveaux Jours* (*42*, III, p.20), and then only as an example of the
risks of using suitcases, this argument, too, does not seem plausible.

That same spring two further manuscripts were submitted for
publication, by the agency of Paulhan, who, by the end of 1942, was
tantamount to being literary director of Les Editions de Minuit (*81*,
p.105). These were *Transcrit du réel*, by Edith Thomas (to be
published in December of that year as *Contes d'Auxois*) and *Les*

---

[5] I am indebted to my printer father for knowledge of printing and for
childhood visits to traditional printing works, and to Jean Périmony for the
publicity material.

Amants d'Avignon, by Elsa Triolet. In Lescure's absence, and as more manuscripts began to arrive, partly due to Paulhan's connections with the CNE (Comité National des Ecrivains), a small selection committee, usually composed of Vercors, Yvonne and the Surrealist poet Paul Eluard sifted through the manuscripts. In the opinion of Vercors and Yvonne, *Transcrit du réel* was far inferior to *Les Amants d'Avignon*, but on his brief return, Lescure accepted the former while rejecting the latter. Vercors says that it was because of his known dislike of Yvonne, which was mutual (*10*, p.198), and that this was the reason Lescure gave him (*10*, p.268). However, Anne Simonin ignores this and suggests that it was because Lescure objected to a deliberate glorification of the Communist Party in it under the term: 'le parti des fusillés'. While it is true that this was Elsa Triolet's intention, and that she had coined the phrase (*71*, p.263), Lescure was not anti-Communist; like Vercors, he was a *compagnon de route*, and, as discussed above, it was probably through Communist contacts that he had obtained *La Pensée libre* (*81*, p.73). Triolet's husband, Louis Aragon, official poet of the Communist Party, had threatened to withhold his next contribution (*Le Musée Grévin*) from Les Editions de Minuit unless *Les Amants d'Avignon* was published (*81*, pp.111–113). Eluard, whom Lescure had left as literary editor, did agree to publish, but in Vercors' accounts, this was because he, like Vercors and others, could not understand Lescure's rejection of it (*10*, p.268; *42*, III, p.30), not because of Aragon's threat; Vercors notes that once Aragon discovered from him that it was Lescure, not the more influential Paulhan, who had refused to publish the text, he withdrew his threat and promised further texts (*42*, III, p.30).

Lescure had left Eluard to keep an eye on Vercors (*81*, p.109), who claims that he positively welcomed the appointment, but dates the rift with Lescure as beginning at this point, and goes on to chart its development (*10*, pp.268–72). This is an excellent example of Vercors giving his own version of the truth in *La Bataille du silence*, as he puts his point of view as tacit defence against Lescure's attacks (See Introduction and Coda: The Post-War History of Les Editions de Minuit). He complains about being abandoned by Lescure (*10*, pp.219–20), so forced to make decisions, but omits to mention that, for at least part of his absence, Lescure had to lie very low, as the Gestapo had smashed the Réseau le Guyon in the Spring of 1942, making twenty-five arrests (*81*, p.62). Although Vercors does admit in *A dire vrai* and in *Les Nouveaux Jours* that Lescure was forced to disappear for three years, he mentions it only to make the point that Lescure left no instructions (*13*, pp. 115–16) and that as Lescure's veto on the distribution of *Le Silence de la mer* was never lifted, this unreasonable situation could not be allowed to continue (*42*, III, pp.58–59). While Lescure may have been unreasonable, the nature of the risks he ran no doubt gave him a different set of priorities from those of Vercors.

It was thanks to Eluard, who had recently re-joined the Communist Party, and to Aragon's increasing influence over him, that the dearth of manuscripts turned into a flood through their Party contacts. The anthology of clandestine poems, *L'Honneur des poètes*, containing one poem by Vercors and three by Aragon, had as its nucleus poems published in the Communist review *Messages*. Like the subject matter of *Chroniques interdites*, this anthology represents the need to react to current events, but Benjamin Péret and other Surrealist poets objected to poetry being used to respond to the real world (*10*, pp.274–75;*76*, pp.114–15). Manuscripts were also received from Mauriac (*Le Cahier noir*), Gide (*Pages de journal*), as well as Aragon's *Le Musée Grévin*. Other contributors during this summer were Léon Motchane, Jacques Debû-Bridel and Charles Morgan. At the end of July apppeared the long-awaited second impression of *Le Silence de la mer*. Vercors remarked resignedly: 'Personne ou presque à Paris n'avait encore lu *le Silence*, tout le monde en parlait, et l'on mélangeait tout. Telle est la destinée des mythes' (*10*, p.278). As an example of the confusion about the book, he related that a friend promised to lend him a 'chef d'oeuvre de Roger Martin du Gard: "Ça s'appelle *Vercors*. Un récit bouleversant"' (ibid).

Although the book may have been almost unread in Paris, in the outside world, unknown to Vercors, the response had been overwhelming. Claude Bellanger had sent a copy to London where it had been reprinted on the personal orders of de Gaulle as the first volume of the series of clandestine texts, *Les Cahiers du silence*; it had been translated into English by Cyril Connolly as *Put Out the Light*, and existed in editions in several countries already, even in Australia and Canada. One night, listening as usual to the BBC, Vercors heard the following appeal from de Gaulle's spokesman, Maurice Schumann: 'Les journaux ne suffisent pas, il faut aussi des livres; j'en appelle à vous, Vercors, encore inconnu et déjà célèbre...' A further surprise soon afterwards was discovering in his garden one morning of a tiny copy of *Le Silence de la mer* printed on India paper; one of millions dropped by the RAF in night sorties all over France, and he was moved to think that his book was being used in this way to boost French morale (*10*, p.279).

In the latter half of 1943 both the rate of production and the organisation of Les Editions de Minuit expanded considerably: extra premises were found for storage, more helpers were enlisted to distribute books round Paris and a professional binder, Vasseur, was recruited, so that Yvonne could at last give up the laborious task of handstitching. A new series of non-fictional books, Témoignages, was begun, in response to *Toulon*, an account received from Yves Farge of the truth behind the controversial sabotaging of the French fleet to prevent it from falling into German hands. Since February 1943, with Lescure's encouragement — he had even contemplated coming out of hiding to discuss progress (*81*, p.108) — Vercors had been writing the story published as *La Marche à l'Etoile* (*10*, pp.296–99). This was a fictionalised homage to his Jewish father and to the Jewish veterans of Verdun, betrayed by Pétain (*84*, pp.140–143; *10*, p.240); he returned to this theme in *L'Imprimerie de Verdun*. The central character, whose dream was to reach Paris and the Pont des Arts, was a conflation of Vercors' father, who had walked to France from his native Hungary, and a friend of his, M. Bernheim, also a Jew and veteran of Verdun, who was nevertheless imprisoned at Drancy then shot as a hostage, not by Germans, but by *gendarmes*. Writing it had been causing Vercors some difficulty, both due to the painful nature of the story and to his attempts to make his style as unlike that of *Le Silence de la mer* as possible to be able to publish it under another pseudonym, which would make it seem that there were plenty of contributors to Les Editions de Minuit. He was unsuccessful in this, as Eluard, who had been given the manuscript as being by a friend of Desvignes-Bruller, immedi-ately recognised the style of Vercors and insisted that it should be published under that name. Published on Christmas Day (to continue the star symbol) 1943, *La Marche à l'étoile* touched a chord among all who were horrified at the Vichy policy against the Jews (see *84*). Their reaction was eloquently expressed in Jean Lescure's review of it for *Les Lettres françaises* (*81*, pp.175–76).

At about the same time he had been working on *Le Songe*, an evocation of the horror of concentration camps inspired by the account of the Oranienburg camp related to him by an escapee, Gérard Chardonne. Vercors' hatred of the Nazis and of the Pétainists dates from this point. So great was his concern to spare the feelings of those who still had relatives who had been deported, that he decided to wait till after the war before publishing it, though it was published in Switzerland on 14 July, 1944 in the journal *Traits*, which took the opposite view that relatives had the right to know (*81*, p.186). The reason that Les Editions de Minuit published Aragon's *Le Musée Grévin*, about Auschwitz, was because Aragon wanted to draw attention to the murders of a hundred Communist women deported in January 1943 (*81*, p.184).

Complete financial independence had been stressed at the outset by Vercors when he arranged to borrow money from Robillard; the editions would not be beholden to Britain or to any organisation for financial support. The efficient sales network among resistance groups meant financial security, but in 1943 Vercors refused the offer of 50,000 francs made by Pierre Brossolette on behalf of the O.C.M. (*Organisation Civile et Militaire*) in return for a printed acknowledgment in all future publications (*10*, p.266, *13* pp.91–92).

The flow of manuscripts continued with John Steinbeck's *The Moon is Down*, which was to be the first volume in the series Voix d'outre-monde, for the works of foreign writers. Other manuscripts received at this time were *Trente-trois sonnets*, composed in prison and memorised for lack of paper by Jean Cassou, and the autobiography of Gabriel Péri, shot by the Germans, sent by Aragon. As this was really a eulogy of the Communist party, it was not admissible. Vercors found the solution by coupling it with extracts from the Catholic author Charles Péguy, publishing it as the *Péguy-Péri*. Vercors's preface to the volume was an opportunity to stress one of his cherished themes, the unity of purpose of those in resistance despite religious and ideological differences (*10*, p.303). Vercors's compromise solution which generated the *Péguy-Péri* is an example of the admirable even-handedness of the editorial committee as a means of dealing with the strong Communist Party influence. Even Anne Simonin, who scrutinises Vercors's actions for any betrayal of his avowed principles, has nothing but praise for this approach, which prevented domination by the Communists: 'L'histoire des rapports Editions de Minuit-PCF est malcommode à écrire. Il ne s'en dégage aucune vérité simple, *et surtout pas celle de la domestication de la maison d'édition par le Parti.* Chaque initiative des communistes — finalement toujours acceptée — appelle un contre-feu...' (*81*, p.127, my emphasis. See also 81, p.81 and p.157). Despite this evidence, Adam Leff claims that Vercors was under Aragon's thumb and could not prevent a Communist takeover of Les Editions de Minuit (*52*, p.713)

The flow of manuscripts increased tremendously during the following spring, and in the space of six weeks thirteen manuscripts were received. In fact, there were more, but Jacques Debû-Bridel's cleaning lady had by mistake burned manuscripts from Jacques Lecompte-Boinet, which he had brought back from Britain in January (*42*, III, p.41). However, Lecompte-Boinet had also brought back copies of the Free French journal *La Marseillaise* containing the serialisation of *Le Silence de la mer* and then, rather strangely, one dated some weeks later, in which the story is castigated as the work of an agent provocateur. This amazing change of attitude, especially considering the eulogies about *Le Silence de la mer* since the first copy was circulated and copied, takes some explaining. Because of the timescale, it is likely, as Anne Simonin suggests (*81*, pp.94–96), that it was due to the editors of the Communist-inspired *Lettres françaises* reacting to de Gaulle's criticism of Communist direct action in 1941. His subsequent adoption of the story, published in London as one of the Cahiers du silence (see 70, pp.222–31) and distributed in the spring of 1943 (hence the copy Vercors found in his garden), was to promote unarmed resistance and bring all resistance under his control. The journalist Ilya Ehrenbourg was given the responsibility of replying from Moscow. It was probably in the autumn of 1943 that his article was published in the USSR and then reprinted in *La Marseillaise* in May 1944:

> …Je ne crois pas qu'ils se soient trouvés en France des hommes assez fous pour composer, imprimer, brocher dans l'illégalité et luxueusement encore, un livre qui s'extasie devant la beauté morale et physique d'un Boche. Si *Le Silence de la mer* fut effectivement imprimé en France, il ne le fut qu'avec l'approbation expresse de Abetz. […] J'ignore si ce livre est venu de France à Londres, je sais qu'il va de Londres en France désorienter et pervertir le lecteur. […] le livre de Vercors fait le jeu des ennemis de la France… (*81*, pp.95–96).

La Marseillaise commented:

> Nous voulons lui [Ilya Ehrenbourg] dire que cet ouvrage nous est effectivement parvenu de la France à Londres dans cette édition luxueuse qui, entre autres raisons, le rend suspect […]. *La Marseillaise* fut la première, dans le monde libre, à reprendre le livre de Vercors. Dès cette époque, nous éprouvions à son sujet des hésitations très proches du jugement d'Ilya Ehrenbourg…(ibid).

Vercors understood that Ehrenbourg's attitude was influenced by being a war correspondent on the Eastern Front, and scorned the comments of the *Lettres françaises* editor, Quilici. After the Liberation, though Ehrenbourg became a friend, Quilici remained hostile to Vercors (42, III, pp.41–42).

It was clear by the spring of 1944 that the course of the war had changed decisively, and there was an air of optimism in the ultimate victory of the Allies, despite the havoc caused, especially to the railways, by intensive Allied bombing. Production at Les Editions de Minuit was at the rate of one new volume per month: in February, Aragon's *Le Crime contre l'esprit,* in March the translation of Steinbeck, published under the title *Nuits noires*, and in April *L'Armistice* by Roger Giron. A comic, but momentarily worrying episode was the attempt by the Germans to undermine the credibility of Les Editions de Minuit by producing a bogus volume: badly printed prophecies culled from Nostradamus foretelling the defeat of the British forces. It would have fooled nobody, and in any case, the Germans could not resolve the paradox of making a supposedly clandestine publication freely available. In the end, having deposited 8,000 copies with the Messageries Hachette, they could not bring themselves to issue the necessary permit for their distribution, and they never saw the light of day (*10*, p.325).

With the Allied invasion in June, and the end of the war in sight, it seemed to Vercors that Les Editions de Minuit had fulfilled its function of combatting the dehumanising influence of Nazism. Now was the moment to focus all attention and efforts on direct action in the coming battle for the liberation of France. In the last weeks of the Occupation Vercors came to realise that he had never been so happy as during these years of war and clandestine activity, which had given him a purpose in life and comradeship which transcended religious and ideological differences. The altruism which had animated the Resistance was coming to an end and personal ambition was beginning to replace the suppression of self-interest for the sake of the common good. Vercors despised those who quickly tried to establish Resistance credentials at the last minute when in fact they had sat on the fence, which in his eyes was tantamount to collaboration. It was decided that only manuscripts already received would be published, and the advertisement for Les Editions de Minuit available in all bookshops, placed in the last number of *Bibliographie de la France*, indicated that the role of the clandestine publishing house was over, though Vercors was prevailed upon, against his better judgement, to allow it to continue (*10*, p.330).

CODA

Reactions to Le Silence de la mer

With the Liberation, Vercors's identity, 'le seul vrai secret de la guerre', according to Aragon, was revealed. His mother simply kissed him in recognition of *La Marche à l'étoile,* while his wife Jeanne seemed rather put out that she had not been let into the secret of his identity. He was delighted at the amazed response of his brother-in-law, Jacques Dennery, when, in answer to Dennery's question 'Qui est Vercors?', he pointed to himself, and in the months following the end of the war, speculation was rife as to what he was like. The heady euphoria was not to last long, and he realised that anonymity had been a pleasure, as the sincerity of a compliment about the unidentified Vercors could not be doubted, unlike the hypocritical flattery to which he was now being subjected. He was awarded the Médaille de la Résistance, was made a member of the Légion d'Honneur and was invited to dinner by de Gaulle, who ignored him. He submitted to becoming a member of the CNE, hitherto having preserved his independence, but felt constrained by arguments that a wrong construction might be put on a refusal. As he feared, he felt like a fish out of water at the first meeting, where Sartre and Camus, whose friendship he had hoped for, were only distantly polite, and Paulhan showed possibly a tinge of jealousy. Debû-Bridel was genuinely pleased at the identity of Vercors, but embarrassed him by saying he was sure to be elected a member of the Académie Française (*10*, 347–50).

With *Le Silence de la mer* Vercors began his career as a writer seeking and expressing in uncompromising terms the truth as he saw it. He tried to come to terms with the dehumanising effects of Nazism in two other short stories, *L'Impuissance* and *Le Songe* and in the novel, *Les Armes de la nuit.* In *Les Animaux dénaturés,* dramatised as *Zoo,* he defined Humanism as the opposite of Nazism. He had hoped that the publication of *PPC* would free him from the label of 'Vercors-qui-brossa-l'écrit-sublime-*Le-Silence-de-la-mer*' (*9*, pp.17–18), but this dogged him all his life. Interviewed by Gilles Plazy in 1990, transcribed as *A dire vrai* (*13*), he is at pains to point out several times his wide range of creative interests and that he was the author of many other books besides the one which everyone links with his name. That Vercors treated it as something which was written to serve a purpose is very clear in a statement made in another interview not long before his death: "Je reste toujours stupéfait de ce que *Le Silence de la mer*, que je considère comme une oeuvre de circonstance, ait obtenu une telle célébrité" (*17*). From my first visit to him in 1987, to the last, shortly before his death in 1991, I always found his self-effacement and his bewilderment at the continuing popularity of the text genuine; he was always happy to get on to more mundane topics of conversation.

However, although Vercors's insistence that it was an oeuvre de circonstance is perfectly valid, the circumstances themselves had changed by the time the first edition reached the general public near the end of 1942. The occupying forces had clearly shown their true nature by that time, thus invalidating Vercors's message, as Sartre points out:

> "Dès la fin de 42, le *Silence de la mer* avait perdu son efficace: c'est que la guerre recommençait sur notre territoire: d'un côté, propagande clandestine, sabotages, déraillements, attentats; de l'autre, couvre-feu, déportations, emprisonnements, tortures, exécutions d'otages.... Nous ne voulions plus savoir si les Allemands qui arrachaient les yeux et les ongles à nos amis étaient des complices ou des victimes du nazisme; en face d'eux il ne suffisait pas de garder un silence hautain... au milieu des bombardements et des massacres, des villages brulés, des déportations, le roman de Vercors semblait une idylle: il avait perdu son public" (*53*, p.121–22).

Apart from this, Sartre criticises the silence of the uncle and niece as evoking the 'mutisme têtu' of Maupassant's peasants, although this would suggest an unthinking obstinacy, not the distinctly unpeasant-like heart-searching of an articulate narrator on whether or not to continue the silence, nor the niece's adamant maintenance of silence despite her emotional turmoil. He also mentions Koestler's criticisms that von Ebrennac and the silence of the uncle and niece are psychologically unconvincing, and that the best that France could offer in the carnage of world war was a fairy story. He disagrees, however, that the German should have been portrayed as a vicious brute, as this would not have reflected contemporary reality (*53*, pp.120–22), which was precisely Vercors's point (see below). What is illustrated by Koestler's views, together with those of Ehrenbourg and the *Marseillaise* editorial, is that because of the particular hallmark of Les Editions de Minuit, favouring literature rather than crude propaganda, it was quite easy to miss the point of the story and allege that it was the work at best of a pacifist, at worst of a collaborator.

It is understandable however, that there should be a feeling that 'real' resistance involved physical action (although it also led to savage reprisals), and James Steel, in the italicised passage which follows, suggests that Vercors was indeed a pacifist: "...s'il préconise une forme de résistance, toute faite en dignité, *il n'en révèle pas moins une attitude remarquablement passive et trahit, dans une certaine mesure, le pacifisme de l'auteur* ainsi que son "internationalisme" illustre le pacifisme d'une bonne partie de l'intelligentsia." (*82*, p. 21, my italics). Classing Vercors as a typical pacifist intellectual, however, certainly does not accord with his own account of his rejection of his earlier belief in Briand's solution of a 'marriage' between France and Germany: "...mais ce n'est guère qu'après l'élection de Hitler et l'émeute fasciste du 6 février que j'ai décidé...qu'il ne suffirait plus d'avoir des opinions, des convictions, mais qu'il fallait tenter de les appliquer (*13*, pp. 20–21). However, because Bruller's initial resolution of applying his anti-Nazi views ('tenter de les appliquer') found its fulfilment in intellectual resistance, that is, fighting Nazism for the control of the mind, he does not advocate armed resistance in *Le Silence de la mer*; even the tenacity of the niece and the violence of von Ebrennac's warnings are simply to raise awareness. However, they make Steel's '*remarquablement* passive' (my italics) something of an exaggeration.

It is certainly possible to identify elements which could be thought of as collaborationist: the silent French people being indoctrinated by a German officer whom the uncle admires, and who is constantly portrayed as very likeable, he and the niece obviously being in love, the lack of a clear propaganda message to resist, and the elegant appearance, as criticised by Ehrenbourg and *La Marseillaise,* perhaps suggesting Vichy or Nazi funding.

James Steel also highlights a point often made by students, that von Ebrennac is too naïve to be true, and he particularly contrasts him with his fiancée of mosquito leg-ripping fame; if she is a typical German, then is von Ebrennac a product of Vercors's humanist imagination (*82*, p.122)? He probably is, but the portrait of the nicest, most un-Nazi like German is deliberately contrived to show that in the end, nice or nasty, they are all the same, because even one of the best of them continues to fight for Hitler, choosing what, in the uncle's eyes, is the easy option by volunteering for the Eastern Front. German soldiers must be seen as representatives of an evil philosophy, not as individuals who, at the time of writing, were being pleasant, and Vercors makes this point with some asperity to Gilles Plazy: '*On vous a reproché cet Allemand trop aimable. —* Mais c'était le thème même de mon récit! Cela n'eût rien signifié que ses hôtes se refusent à lui s'il s'était montré grossier ou agressif!' (*13*, p.32). In fact, von Ebrennac is not entirely naïve — Vercors makes him admit that he knows that the senior Nazis are like his fiancée (p. 40), but this is a device to lead into the presentation of the Briand-inspired argument that France will heal Germany, so that through von Ebrennac's later disillusionment it can be demolished as no longer valid.

However, criticisms of von Ebrennac by Koestler, Sartre, James Steel and others are right: he, like the niece, is a two-dimensional character representing an extreme position, just like Camus' Meursault — does anyone really believe in him, or that a

European would have been guillotined in 1942 for killing an Arab? Yet, like *Le Silence de la mer*, *L'Etranger* is thought-provoking as well as extremely successful. Both use fictional characters to present a message, thus appealing to the imagination and so enhancing their symbolic value for doctrinaire purposes, which is a common use of stories and one exploited by Vichy propaganda (see Foreword to *78*, p.v). It is Vercors's gift for storytelling, as I argue in the next chapter, which carries most readers along, so that their critical faculties are to some extent suspended, thus leaving them more receptive to his message.

Oudeville's remark: "Pourquoi *Le Silence de la mer*? Moi je dirais plutôt le silence de la nièce" (*10*, p.203)' caused Vercors to add the short passage on p.55, explaining the hidden tumult in the depths of the sea as a clue to the significance of the title, realising that in his desire to avoid propaganda, his message had perhaps been too enigmatic. William Kidd sees Oudeville's remark as flippant and based on word play: "nièce" suggesting by analogy "mère", not "mer" (*49*, pp.38–39). He further justifies this by saying that, as students confuse the uncle with a father, this implies an absent mother. This premise is very fragile; while fathers and daughters, rather than uncles and nieces tend to live under the same roof, I can see no reason not to take the relationship at face value. This more distanced relationship than that of a father gives the uncle more credibility as narrator (see *Facets of the Text*: Narration), as he is able to comment more objectively on von Ebrennac's loaded comments and looks in his niece's direction and on her physical appearance and emotions, even when she is under great strain. When I asked Vercors why he had chosen this relationship, he replied that it just seemed natural, and that he didn't really know. Oudeville's question is in fact very pertinent, as there was no reference to the sea in the version he was commenting on, and the only silence was that of the niece. Moreover, Oudeville would be far more aware of the shape of words than of the sound of them; day after day, he did everything from setting up type to proof reading the resulting text, and would do it accurately, as mistakes could not, as we have seen, be rectified at the tap of a key. It is therefore inconceivable that he would have mistaken 'mer' for 'mère'.

Despite the problem of the late appearance of *Le Silence de la mer* and doubts concerning its Resistance-worthiness, it still continues to fascinate. One of the reasons is the revival of interest in the Occupation, particularly since the 1980's, and it is currently a fast growing area of academic study. In France, one of the main catalysts was Marcel Ophuls's film "*Le Chagrin et la pitié*", part of the 1968 revolt against de Gaulle, and seeking to demythologise his image of the majority of France united behind the Resistance. The continuing Gaullist promotion of *Le Silence de la mer* as a paradigm of the Resistance (*44*, p.63), where the dignified refusal to acknowledge the enemy blankets the complexities and nastiness (*44*, p.67), played its part in this (*44*, p.3). Reconciliation, too, was a post-war priority for de Gaulle, and Vercors was dismayed that, unlike him, he refused to condemn publishers who had collaborated (*81*, pp.239–40). In *Le Chagrin et la pitié*, Ophuls took delight in painting the opposite picture to the Gaullist myth, that of a population which largely collaborated; the truth, unsurprisingly, lies not in black and white terms, but in shades of grey. Although the film was released in 1971, it was so iconoclastic that permission was not given till 1981 for it to be televised. Louis Malle's film of amoral collaboration, *Lacombe Lucien* (1974), also discredited the Gaullist myth (*69*, pp.1–2). De Gaulle had insisted that as the Vichy 'government' was no such thing (*69*, p.134), the Fifth Republic had never ceased to exist; it therefore required much effort and the revelation of many shades of grey, including about Mitterrand, to bring about Chirac's apology in 1995 on behalf of the French government for the Vichy government's persecution of the Jews (*74*, pp.41–50). However, the long-term protection of the ringleaders meant that the only subsequent trials were of scapegoats: Paul Touvier in 1994 and Maurice Papon in 1997 (84, pp.278–306 *69*, pp.354–81). Demyth-ologising sometimes went too far, as in the case of attacks on the Resistance record of the Aubracs and of Jean Moulin (*69*, p.631).

Margaret Atack identifies a further reason for the continued fascination of and with the text: the ring of truth which stems from its being "littérature de témoignage"; apart from the subject matter and that it was elegantly presented literature, the fact that it was produced in difficult circumstances made it part of the struggle against the enemy, thus equating "littérature de témoignage" with "littérature de combat". The reader, too, became part of the struggle by taking a risk through acquiring the text, and by working with the author to interpret it and apply it to current events (*44*, pp.23–26). We have seen Vercors's commitment to this *témoignage* in his willingness to adapt his subject matter to the changing face of the Occupation in *Chroniques interdites*, the *Péguy-Péri* and *L'Honneur des poètes*; *Les Mots* and *L'Impuissance* are other examples. Despite the violence of some of the sentiments, they were still expressed in the controlled manner which was the hallmark of Les Editions de Minuit.

In the play version of *Le Silence de la mer*, first performed in 1949 (directed by Jean Mercure), Vercors took the opportunity of introducing a more obvious tone of resistance, first, through the statement: 'Il est beau pour un soldat de désobéir aux ordres criminels' (*7*, p.23), followed by discussion with the uncomprehending von Ebrennac, and secondly, through a rifle hidden by the uncle, whose symbolism is made clearer in the 1990 version directed by Jean Périmony, because of the uncle's and niece's joyful expressions as they contemplate it (*7*, p.24). Vercors asserts that if *Le Silence de la mer* had been written nearer the time of its publication, then it would certainly have contained a call to arms: 'L'aurais-je écrit un ou deux ans plus tard, je ne me serais plus contenté de cette résistance passive, en attente d'autre chose. Si "l'oncle" eût été alors en âge de participer à la résistance, il aurait sûrement pris les armes contre l'occupant' (Letter to Ethel Tolansky, 11–4–84, *45*, p.364). Detailed treatment of the play can be found in *49*, pp.47–49; *82*, pp.191–96, pp.361–64.

Apart from *Le Silence de la mer*, few clandestine novella or short stories were re-published after the Liberation, because they were not of sufficient literary merit to stand independently of the context of "témoignage". In 1948, with the war still fresh in people's memories, Vercors could claim that *Le Silence de la mer* was still very popular because it was an *oeuvre de circonstance*.: "....Je ne jouerai pas les modestes jusqu'à prétendre que ce livre n'a pas les qualités qu'on lui prête: mais son extraordinaire succès n'est pas dû à ses seules qualités. Il est dû aux circonstances." (*Les lettres françaises*, no.205, 22 avril, and no.206, 9 avril, 1948, quoted in *81*, p.205). However, although some sixty years later, the *oeuvre de circonstance* argument is no longer valid, the work continues to fascinate long after its post-Liberation glow has faded. This is partly explained by the resurgence of popular and academic interest in the Occupation since *Le Chagrin et la pitié* and since official records have been released. However, a counterpart to this analysis and demythologising, now that few survivors of the period remain, is a desire for celebration through the fuelling of collective memory. The fiftieth anniversary of the publication of *Le Silence de la mer*, 25th February, 1992, was the occasion of the unveiling of the plaques to Vercors and Jacques Lecompte-Boinet at the Left Bank end of the Pont des Arts (see above: Les Editions de Minuit), the location a tribute to *La Marche à L'Etoile*. In his eulogy, Maurice Schumann made clear the purpose of collective memory for future generations: Adolescent du prochain millénaire, ne traverse pas en courant, les yeux baissées, cette passerelle qui te rend visible la continuité de ton histoire; garde le temps d'une longue pensée pour les volontaires sans lesquels cette histoire ne serait plus vraiment à toi!' (*16*). In 1995, the first international conference on Bruller/Vercors, together with an exhibition of his graphic art, was another way of celebrating his importance. The 1990's were also the time of particularly notable presentations of the play version of *Le Silence de la mer*; in 1990, by Jean Périmony, mentioned above, and in 1999 it was performed in Paris by the Bécard company as part of the celebrations of the centenary of the birth of the Resistance leader, Jean Moulin, and had such an effect on audiences of all ages that its run was greatly extended.

Despite all this, without its literary qualities, the play would probably not still be performed, and the *récit* would be little more than a historical curiosity. It is Vercors's appeal to the imagination (*45*, pp.139–46) through his skilful exploitation of literary techniques, examined in the next chapter, which gives it a resonance irrespective of its historical context and accounts for its continuing appeal.

The Post-War History of Les Editions de Minuit

No other clandestine publishing house came anywhere near the importance or range of Les Editions de Minuit, publishing about twenty titles by the end of the war: 'Nulle part en Europe occupée, les Editions de Minuit n'eurent de réel equivalent; elles qui furent, non pas le réceptacle, mais le creuset de la résistance des écrivains demeurés sur le sol français, inventant à leur usage une forme spécifique de «résistance civile», la «littérature clandestine». L'aventure était à hauts risques, elle fut et demeure une expérience singulière' (*81*, p.196). Despite his view that the task of les Editions de Minuit had been accomplished, Vercors was swayed by his wife and by Eluard, Yvonne Paraf and Aulard to continue, and in the autumn of 1945 it became a limited company with Vercors as managing director and Yvonne as deputy, although it had been operating under commercial rules for a year already. In her study of much hitherto unknown archive material, Anne Simonin notes that after the war a myth quickly grew up which made Vercors and resistance synonymous, and in her quest to show another side to Vercors, she discusses Lescure's accusations and the post-war fortunes of Les Editions de Minuit.

The tensions between Vercors and Lescure continued, and in a letter written in Switzerland on 7 October, 1944 to his wife and daughter (*81*, pp.212–13), Lescure made many criticisms of Vercors, and showed his dislike of Yvonne. He showed something of a mania for 'purity' by criticising them for claiming working expenses, although both had given up their jobs by this time, and were asking for very modest sums, but his point was that true patriots would not try to make money out of resistance. In his diary, he noted Vercors's reply that in the *maquis* Lescure would have received food and lodging, noting also his own tart rejoinder that straw for bedding does not cost much (see *72*, p.100, for a similar view of life in the *maquis*). He also refused shares which Vercors had offered him in the company, and he felt that those like himself, who had actually borne arms, had been the real fighters, but were now losing out to the intellectuals. His greatest reproach to 'J.B.' was that he had turned Les Editions de Minuit into big business — on the contrary, however, Vercors was always the most poorly-paid employee, and his rather hard-line idealism contributed to the financial problems of the company. Lescure was undoubtedly generous, contributing money to Les Editions de Minuit anonymously, and a note found in his papers confirmed that works bearing the inscription 'au dépens d'un patriote' had been paid for by Lescure. However, he was in the fortunate position of being able to live off the sale of his uncle's library (*81*, p.214), and showed a less than understanding attitude towards Vercors's and Yvonne's precarious personal financial situations.

In the same letter from Switzerland, he said that he had refused to join the *Conseil littéraire* of Les Editions de Minuit because he felt that Bruller and Yvonne had taken over and changed its tone. He claimed that the publishing venture had been his brainchild, not Bruller's: '...j'ai pris la décision de créer des livres qui pourraient permettre aux écrivains français de s'exprimer au milieu de cette nuit fabriquée par les maîtres de guerre...' (Lecture prononcée en Suisse,1944, Archives Célia Bertin, *81,* p. 69). According to Vercors, (*9*, p.20; *13*, p.116; *42*, III, pp.60–62), Lescure's condition for re-joining Les Editions de Minuit was for Yvonne to leave. He further claimed in a Genevan review that he and Célia Bertin, with whom he had fallen in love, were the joint founders of Les Editions de Minuit, though Anne Simonin could find no record of this article (*81*, p.211). Vercors realised that Lescure was putting his loyalty to the test over Yvonne, and was saddened at his lack of integrity. He assumed that this was in revenge for preparing to publish Jacques Debû-Bridel's *Historique des Editions de minuit* in 1945, without being able to consult Lescure, absent in Switzerland, although, in fact, Vercors had asked Debû-Bridel to 'faire briller Lescure à toutes les pages. Afin d'éviter un nouvel incident entre nous' (*42*, III, p.61). However, this stratagem provoked an angry reaction from Lescure on receipt of the proofs from Vercors (*42*, III, p.61). In Mme Debû-Bridel's opinion, Lescure was suffering from persecution mania, while Edith Thomas thought that he was on the verge of a nervous breakdown (*81*, p. 219). He refused to see Vercors, and broke with Les Editions de Minuit in the autumn of 1945. Vercors understood that Lescure's attacks on him could be partly explained by the effects of persecution by the Dominicans when he was a devout young man. He had passed on reports of the sexual depravity of his spiritual mentor, but his superiors closed ranks and forced him from the editorship of the Roman Catholic periodical *La Revue des jeunes*. He opened the bookshop where Bruller met him (see *Introduction*), but again, was a victim of the Dominicans' conspiracy against him, and was forced to close it in 1932 (*10*, pp.130–31; *81*, pp.39–44). Vercors also understood not only about the deprivations Lescure had suffered in the *maquis* (see above), but also about terrible examples of Nazi reprisals he had witnessed (*42*, III, p.59).

Lescure's departure from Les Editions de Minuit was unfortunate not only because it was acrimonious, and affected Vercors all his life (see *Introduction*), but also because it deprived Vercors and Yvonne of his expertise and his contacts in the world of publishing, where events were to show that they were inexperienced, and that Vercors's unease about the wisdom of allowing Les Editions de Minuit to continue after the war was well-founded. While, as the undisputed 'maison d'édition de la Résistance' during the Occupation, it had given voice to writers of conscience who would not otherwise have been heard, it no longer had any obvious role, and its reputation rested retrospectively on being 'né de la guerre', a position reinforced by the very speedy publication of Debu-Bridel's *Historique* (*81*, p.216).

Vercors felt strongly that writers who in his view had collaborated with the enemy should be censured because they were responsible for the consequences of the thoughts expressed in their writing (*Carrefour*, 16.2.45, quoted in *79*, p.28). He joined the Commission de l'Epuration de l'Edition and the Commission de l'Epuration de la C.N.E, resigning from the former because he felt that other members were compromising their principles, and again taking a hard line by supporting the latter's decision to publish a blacklist of authors who had given any material or moral help to the

enemy. Others disagreed, including Paulhan, who had maintained a
foot in both camps, and who felt that writers had the right to make
mistakes. As Vercors naturally applied his draconian criteria to
selecting texts for Les Editions de Minuit, this had the effect of
drastically reducing the number of authors whose work he was
prepared to publish — on the other hand, however, he found himself
unable to refuse texts from anyone with an unblemished Resistance
record regardless of literary quality, not even feeling it necessary to
read them before agreeing to publish. The entire corpus of texts was,
therefore, often of indifferent quality and about the war or politics.
Sales figures were consequently low, except for Vercors's own
books, which accounted for a third to a half of sales until the early
1950s, showing the continuing magic of the name at least amongst
those who wished to keep alive the Resistance myth. However, as
many bookshop owners had been supporters of the Vichy régime,
they saw no reason to promote books published by Les Editions de
Minuit, while to Vercors's chagrin, books by former collaborators
sold well (*81*, pp.282–83). It was human nature now that the
Occupation was over to forget about it and get back to normal, and
while many saw the point of collaborators being punished during the
épuration, though not necessarily approving of the associated
vengeance, the rationale and definition of literary *épuration* were
more difficult to grasp — in fact it proved impossible for the
Commission de l'Epuration de la C.N.E. to define a 'crime contre
l'esprit', its criterion for literary collaboration with the enemy (*81*,
p.233).

Yvonne shared Vercors's high ideals which, together with lack
of business experience, rather blinded them to commercial reality:
"Dès le départ, les Editions de Minuit légales ne se conçoivent pas
comme une entreprise, inévitablement soumise à des critères de
rentabilité mais comme la poursuite d'une aventure commune. Moins
vendeuses que gardiennes d'un temple ou brûlerait l'esprit de la
Résistance." (*81,* p.245). The firm had entered the post-war era with
quite a healthy profit of 300,000 francs at the Liberation, because
after 1943, publications were sold directly instead of by the wartime
method of subscription. However, because of the insistence on

financial independence, so that no party or Resistance group would
have any control or influence, it had no financial backing.
Inefficiency added to the existing problems — manuscripts were
often lost or forgotten about, so that authors became tired of waiting
and went elsewhere (*81*, p.248). However, a further reason for the
slow rate of publishing, and one which was not Vercors' fault, was
the the problem of paper, which was divided among publishing
houses according to how much they had used before the war, when of
course Les Editions de Minuit did not officially exist. Though Anne
Simonin quotes Vercors's complaint in *Les Nouveaux jours* about the
unfairness of this (*42*, III, p.58 quoted in *81*, p.240), she does not say
that it slowed down production. Vercors is even more explicit about
this in *A dire vrai*:

> " ....Donc, mes amis, bravo Vercors, bravo les Editions
> de Minuit, mais pas de papier pour vous. Il a fallu
> l'intervention scandalisée de Malraux[6] pour nous en faire
> attribuer quelques rames... Gallimard, en plus des
> attributions officielles, en regorgeait dans ses caves; nous
> en avions si peu que nous ne pouvions pas, et de très
> loin, imprimer nos ouvrages au même rythme; nos
> auteurs devaient donc parfois attendre un an, voire deux;
> alors que chez Gallimard ils seraient imprimés dans les
> trois mois. A part quelques fidèles, ils s'envolaient tous
> là où ils pouvaient paraître (*13*, pp.102–03).

The firm now occupied commercial premises instead of being based
in Yvonne's flat, moving first to the rue St-Placide, then to the
Boulevard St-Germain in 1946, but it was too insignificant to have a
special deal with major distributors, although it became part of the
group "Pour le Livre", which united the few publishing houses which
had refused any collaboration.

Still mindful of political independence, Vercors refused to join
Aragon's "Bibliothèque Française" because of its Communist

---

[6] De Gaulle did not intervene, in Vecors's opinion, because Vercors had
refused OCM support (*42*, III, p.54).

leanings. He also deliberately shunned any cooperation with Gallimard because of its collaboration during the Occupation. Jean Lescure, who was beginning to have a revitalising effect as literary editor, earned Vercors's disapproval for agreeing with Gallimard to publish some texts which they were too busy to publish, and left shortly afterwards (*81*, pp.257–58). There followed many other disagreements between Vercors and staff members, mainly because of Vercors's strong views, but also because he was not good at delegating responsibility although he was often absent. However, Anne Simonin reads into Vercors's comment: "déjà bien trop occupé par mille taches, parmi lesquelles la direction des Editions de Minuit" (*42*, III, p.100), that he found running the publishing firm too onerous (*81*, p. 248), whereas it would seem to show simply that he had too many irons in the fire. As it was, he felt that he had to keep his hands firmly on the reins to prevent the firm from being tainted by former collaborators, and this led to confrontation and his subsequent resignation.

To many former *résistants*, the firm's lack of commercial success was a kind of guarantee of integrity, and various rescue schemes were initiated, including shares with a 5,000 franc deposit and subscriptions to "Les Amis des Editions de Minuit" (*81*, p.287). More substantial help came with the appointment to the staff of Jérome Lindon and the consequent injection of capital by his father-in-law, Marcel Rosenfeld. In an attempt to look to the future, books on science and technology were published and people with no Resistance background were taken on — Georges Bataille even had strong fascist sympathies. Despite this loosening of ties with the past, between 1946 and 1948 profits were halved, and only 20 titles a year were being published. Rosenfeld invested more capital, and the majority of shares were now held by people with no Resistance connection — Vercors, with his low salary, could not afford to buy more shares to redress the balance. The Resistance was fading from most people's memory, and Vercors seemed no longer protected by his reputation — there was a campaign to discredit his wartime rôle, particularly in Paulhan's *De la Paille et du grain*, (Gallimard, Paris, 1948). Vercors and Yvonne gave up as directors, though Vercors

wanted to exert moral influence and have the right of veto (*81*,
pp.323–24). In 1949 Vercors severed his links with Les Editions de
Minuit, withdrawing his books, and he and Lindon entered into
litigation, abandoned in 1950 (*81*, pp.327–34 and see *Introduction*).
Lindon did not share Vercors's own view of himself as the
incarnation of Les Editions de Minuit (he had threatened to remove
the name when he left), and when Vercors wrote to him in 1954 to
say that he had not always approved of his editorial stance, but now
did, he replied that Vercors's opinion was irrelevant to him (*81*,
pp.466–67). Georges Lambrichs, as literary director, reversed
Vercors's policy of non-cooperation with Gallimard by exploiting his
links with Paulhan, leading to the publication of the review *84*, thus
ending the literary isolation of les Editions de Minuit. Lambrichs
resigned in 1954 after a breakdown of relations with Lindon (*81*,
pp.446–53).

1954 was a watershed for Les Editions de Minuit — a combination of circumstances and personalities enabled its languishing
reputation and commercial fortunes (near bankruptcy in 1953) to be
turned round. In 1954, too, an amnesty was declared for
collaborators — the appointment in 1955 of one of the *nouveau
roman* writers, Alain Robbe-Grillet, as *conseiller littéraire* might not
have been possible earlier, as he came from a strongly anti-semitic
pétainiste background (*81*, pp.459–61). His influence was decisive
for the future — *La Modification* by fellow *nouveau roman* author,
Michel Butor (Eds. de Minuit, 1957), won the firm's first public
success with the *Prix Renaudot*, and in his thirty-year stay, Robbe-
Grillet consolidated its reputation for publishing *avant-garde*
literature. Lindon had already published the review *Critique*, which
included articles by Butor and Robbe-Grillet, and had also risked
publishing texts by the unknown Samuel Beckett, so that Les
Editions de Minuit was seen to be on the cutting edge of
experimental literature. Lindon was also anxious to maintain the
intellectual resistance tradition of "la pureté spirituelle de l'homme"
with political *engagement,* but in the separate "Documents" series,
under the historian Pierre Vidal-Naquet. Powerful texts against the
Algerian War like *Pour Djamila Bouhired* (G. Arnaud and J. Vergès,

Eds. de Minuit, 1957), together with the *Déclaration sur le droit à l'insoumission dans la guerre d'Algérie*, (nicknamed, because of the 121 signatories, including Vercors's[7], the "Manifeste des 121"), earned for Les Editions de Minuit a reputation for political subversion (*81*, p.470).

Lindon's great achievement was the separation of literature from texts of *engagement*, acknowledging that authors could be politically committed as individuals, yet write literary works for purely aesthetic reasons. He correctly foresaw that this policy, which he maintained till his death in 2001, would win for Les Editions de Minuit a distinctive niche in the publishing world: "L'image des Editions de Minuit qui se dégage du "Manifeste des 121" est claire: modernité en littérature et fer de lance dans les combats du siècle. Articuler, sans confondre, rupture esthétique et insoumission politique contribuera à démultiplier le potentiel de subversion des Editions de Minuit et leur conférera une position d'avant-garde quasi-inexpugnable dans le monde de l'édition." (*81*, p.471).

---

[7] Vercors wrote to de Gaulle, returning his insignia of the *Légion d'Honneur* in protest, and was mocked for it in the satirical periodical *Le Canard enchaîné* (*9*, p.356). He later dates his decision to leave public life (see Introduction) from that moment, if that was what people thought of him (*42*, III, pp.311–12).

2. Facets of the Text

Literary Techniques

'Pas précisement un peintre, comme il n'est pas précisement un poète [...] L'intention de Vercors n'est pas là où ils la cherchent [...] Elle est entre l'oeil et le coeur, ou les littérateurs, si malins, osent rarement s'aventurer.' Although Stanislas Fumet wrote these words as a preface to *Les Armes de la nuit* (*Caliban,* May 1948), his comments about the elusive nature of Vercors's artistry could equally well apply to *Le Silence de la mer.* As with Joseph Conrad, whom Vercors acknowledged as an enormous influence, it is an artistry of suggestion, clues, ambiguity, in which meaning is conveyed and secrets are betrayed by gestures, facial expressions and silences. Conrad's explanation of his aims in the preface to *The Nigger of the Narcissus* also holds good for Vercors:

> Fiction, if it at all aspires to be art — appeals to temperament [...] Such an appeal to be effective must be an impression conveyed through the senses; [...], because temperament, whether individual or collective, is not amenable to persuasion. All art, therefore, appeals primarily to the senses, and the artistic aim when expressing itself in written words must also make its appeal through the senses if its high desire is to reach the secret spring of responsive emotions. (55, p.xli)

Conrad's identification of the importance of the senses in creating a response accords with Fumet's verdict that Vercors succeeded in aiming 'entre l'oeil et le coeur', that is, in appealing to the imagination and feelings of the reader (*45*, pp.139–46). A response implies choice of interpretation on the part of the individual reader, as

Vercors wrote to me: 'vous savez aussi que le sens donné par l'auteur
à ce qu'il écrit n'est pas plus valable que celui de ses lecteurs, *étant
donnée l'ambiguïté foncière de toute pensée et donc de son
expression'* (*85*, my emphasis). The techniques which Vercors used
to create a response from the reader form the subject of this chapter.

Narration

Vercors, like Conrad, filters his story throu
apparently artless technique being a highly sub
to select exactly what he wishes to present to
narrators, like the uncle in *Le Silence de la mer,* tell their story in a
conversational manner. The uncle acts as the reader's eyes and ears,
and because, like Conrad's Marlow, he is also a participant in the
events, a natural commentator, blending into the background and
becoming a kind of *porte-parole* of the average Frenchman. At the
outset a bond is created with fellow-sufferers under the Occupation
by the disparaging remarks made about the two German soldiers, not
only about their physical appearance ('dégingandé et maigre' and
'carré, aux mains de carrier' (p.19) but also their attempts at French
('Ils me parlèrent, dans ce qu'ils supposaient être du français', ibid).
The shared laughter, as in Texcier's *Conseils à l'occupé,* reinforces
the bond. Vercors has, therefore, like Conrad, created a narrator who
has slipped in almost unnoticed. The uncle observes the scene in
what appears a perfectly natural way as he lives his daily life.
However, because he and his niece are in the midst of the extreme
situation of having an enemy soldier billeted on them, it seems
equally natural that he should feel moved to comment on it. Vercors
has found a plausible reason to set most of the uncle's observations
in the evening, when von Ebrennac joins them after his day's duties
are over. Naturally enough, the uncle is at leisure to sit in his
comfortable armchair, smoking his pipe. As the image of the pipe-
smoker is conducive to the idea of a certain impassivity, of observing
the scene and musing on it, this easily lends a natural air of reflective
conversation to the uncle's narration. The household routine of
evening coffee ('elle venait de me servir mon café, comme chaque
soir', p.21) has its conversational corollary ('le café me fait dormir',

ibid), which has the effect of the narrator chatting to the reader. Although interrupted by the officer's arrival, the routine continues nevertheless: the uncle calmly carries on drinking his coffee, then lights his pipe. Equally, the niece resumes drinking the coffee she had left to show the officer the way upstairs ('elle reprit sa tasse et continua de boire son café', p.23). She too has been introduced in a natural way in the context of routine evening activities: as well as partaking of the ritual cup of coffee, she has been mending, and we see later that it is her habit to sew or knit in the evenings. Our initial introduction to her is made in a conversational manner ('ce fut ma nièce qui alla ouvrir quand on frappa' p.21), and her disapproval of the officer's intrusion is manifested by her rigidity, silence and refusal to meet his eyes. The uncle notes in a matter-of-fact way that she then resumes her coffee and her invisible mending; it is clear, however, that this is a sign of her dogged desire to behave as if nothing had happened. The fact that the officer has interrupted a way of life which nevertheless continues, despite his presence in the house, is underlined by the coffee-drinking routine: 'Il revint le soir à a veille. Nous prenions notre café' (p.25). For his ses what had become his accustomed hour: 'à idé nos tasses' (p.48). This technique of linking the events of the story with the elements of day-to-day routine is a skilful exploitation of the manner in which people commonly relate events in real life, enhancing the natural feel of the narrative. Furthermore, once these elements have been established, they can then be used as a pretext for significant incidents in the plot. We know that the uncle is a pipe smoker, and it is because he goes upstairs for tobacco that he thinks it is his niece he hears playing the harmonium (p.35). We know too that he sits in a deep armchair (p.27), and, on the occasion of von Ebrennac's last visit, he gives this as the reason that his eyes were on a level with the officer's hand, so that he could observe the tell-tale signs of agitation (p.51).

As the tale progresses, the uncle and niece find that von Ebrennac has become an indispensable part of their routine, and one of the most touching aspects of the story is their struggle to maintain 'normality' while the officer increasingly affects them and occupies their thoughts to the extent that they miss him if he does not turn up at his 'usual' time (p.26). Although the externals remain the same, like the evening cup of coffee, the uncle's pipe-smoking and the decision to continue to leave the connecting door unlocked, we see clearly that life has been altered. For instance, the niece pretends to be absorbed in knitting or sewing to show that she is ignoring von Ebrennac, but it very soon becomes apparent that her mind is not on her work, her manual dexterity deteriorating from the skill required for invisible mending (p.23) to the 'travail absurde' of winding a ball of wool, 'le seul sans doute qui pût encore s'accorder à son attention abolie' (p.52). She knits 'lentement, d'un air très appliqué' (p.26), the expression 'd'un air' betraying that the uncle suspects that she, too, is wondering where the officer is; she knits with 'une vivacité mécanique' (p.27) because she is embarrassed when he comes to warm himself; she breaks the thread, no doubt through pulling too hard, when he talks of his fiancée, taking a long time needle beneath his gaze (p.40); and she is too tired an work when she guesses that her uncle has seen von Eb

The daily routine thus has the twofold function of anchoring the story in real life, creating the link between the fictional tale and the message it embodies, but also serving to focus the story on the person of von Ebrennac, whose presence and absence increasingly make the daily routine appear hollow — a question of going through the motions while their minds are on him: 'L'avouerai-je? Cette absence ne me laissait pas l'esprit en repos [je voyais bien, à l'application têtue qu'elle mettait soudain à son ouvrage [...] qu'elle non plus n'était pas exempte de pensées pareilles aux miennes' (p.47).

As Conrad so often does, Vercors employs a second narrator to alter the perspective and allow different aspects of the story to be related in a natural way. Part of the technique of making the reader feel sympathetic towards the officer is to make him less a German enemy and more a human being, portraying him with effective touches like feeling the cold (p.26), rubbing his head (p.28), speaking considerately to his hosts (pp.22, 29, 39) and through his unfailingly courteous behaviour, while the natural pretext of warming himself at the fire (p.26) leads to his talking about the difference between winters at home and in France. In a similarly natural way the uncle prepares the reader for the revelation of von Ebrennac's feelings by remarking that they had come to expect him to talk about what was important to him (p.30). Briand's unrealised vision of a united France and Germany is thus presented through the officer's recollections, together with his reasons for his attachment to France, and it is again through his eyes that Vercors conveys his message about the impossibility of reconciliation with Germany while the Nazis are still in power.

Because von Ebrennac makes it clear how much he adores France and this French house, it is natural that he should look at objects in the room, or wander round touching and looking. This adds to the impression that he is becoming integrated with the family and with France, so that we feel more his pain and disillusionment at the end. It also leads plausibly to his noticing and commenting on the books in the room and this glorification of French culture, with the message to writers that it is virtually synonymous with literature, prepares us for Vercors's warning in the final scene that the Nazis intend to stamp out French literature. The fact that the uncle as first narrator filters von Ebrennac as second narrator, who in turn filters the words and attitudes of his former friends, allows Vercors to portray this final scene with great power and with great appeal to the imagination. We are aware of the uncle's feelings and his pain at his niece's suffering, as well as being aware of what the niece herself is having to bear. We also see and hear the uncle's perception of von Ebrennac's anguish, which reinforces von Ebrennac's own narration of the violent mockery of his Nazi colleagues. In this crucial dénouement, Vercors has been careful to avoid the overtones of propaganda which might have arisen if he had chosen to give von Ebrennac a long harangue. Instead, he keeps us in horrified fascination due to the counterpoint of the uncle's narration, von Ebrennac's narration and the words of the Nazi officers, in a repeated sequence. James Steel suggests that Vercors's decision to have von Ebrennac quote his fellow officers is a way of sparing his compatriots the pain they would have felt if the mockery had been reported through the lips of the (French) uncle (*82*, p.128), but it is hard to see this episode as anything but extremely painful. An alternative treatment is found in Jean-Pierre Melville's film; while Vercors judged it a very faithful adaptation, he felt that the sustained suspense in the novella, beginning with von Ebrennac's descending footsteps, was broken by transferring the scene to Paris and putting the insults and revelations into the mouths of his fellow officers: '...la seule exception (et à mon avis, regrettable) c'est le voyage d'Ebrennac (sic) à Paris, où on voit et entend discuter avec ses amis nazis. Ce qui d'une part n'est pas compatible avec le récit de l'oncle, lequel n'a pas évidemment assisté à la scène, et d'autre part brise la discrétion dudit récit'(*85*). This and other aspects of the film are discussed in *49*, pp.45–47.

   Vercors's use of a narrator who is not omniscient, a device Conrad frequently used, has the effect of intriguing the reader by its indeterminacy. The uncle knows nothing of von Ebrennac except for the portion of his life covered by the narration, with the effect that, at the end, no loose ends are tied up, the 'ending' simply consisting of the departure of the officer, leaving the uncle, niece and reader in limbo. This mirrors the prevailing mood of uncertainty of the Occupation, lending weight to Vercors's implied message. He has skilfully led up to it by changing the tone of the narration, prefaced by the pessimistic symbolism of the quotation from *Othello*, and through von Ebrennac's grim words and attitude, leaving the reader in no doubt that he is referring to contemporary events. If there were any doubt, the use of the future tense in 'vers ces plaines immenses où le blé futur *sera* nourri de cadavres (my emphasis) would resolve it.

   Furthermore, the ambiguity produced by the occasional vagueness of the uncle has the effect of engaging our attention, involving the reader in an attempt to decode the clues, to weigh up the relative merits of a variety of possibilities and thus to try to get to the truth of a situation. In the first awkward silence with von Ebrennac, we wonder what he is trying to say by his gesture which the uncle fails to understand (p.23). We try to visualise more closely his physical appearance, because the uncle is not at first sure of the colour of his eyes (pp.22,24). 'Je ne sais si…' makes us wonder with the uncle if von Ebrennac deliberately took the stair into the kitchen (p.24), while the use of the phrase later concentrates our attention on the tone, scornful or otherwise, of the Nazi officers (p.53). Similar locutions are used: 'je ne suis pas sûr', 'il se peut que' (p.25), 'sans doute' (pp.26, 30, 52). Alternative interpretations are offered: 'était-ce pour nous épargner la vue de l'uniforme ennemi? Ou pour nous le faire oublier […] Les deux, sans doute' (p.30). 'Pourquoi' is used effectively, its repetition increasing the suspense as the uncle asks himself why the officer is waiting for a reply this time (p.50). When the uncle finally says 'Entrez, monsieur', he immediately asks 'Pourquoi ajoutai-je: monsieur?' (p.50). Again, alternative explanations are offered, this sequence underlining the enormous step he has taken in talking to the officer. In the same scene, effective use is made of the repetition of 'je crus' as the uncle watches and listens attentively to von Ebrennac, so that we strain our ears to hear him laugh (p.54), and strain our eyes to see a glimpse of a smile (p.58), while at the end our emotions are engaged as we wait to see if he will rebel or succumb (p.57), or if the niece will finally speak (p.59).

The uncle's quandary about his behaviour towards von Ebrennac, skilfully conveyed in a range of contradictory feelings and impulses, was intended to address the consciences of French readers of the time and to make them ask themselves awkward questions about their attitude to the occupiers. The uncle does not, for example, show deference by standing up when the officer arrives (p.22), but is impressed by his politeness nevertheless (p.23). He is annoyed to find himself worried as he thinks of him in the snow (p.26) and notes that von Ebrennac never sat down in their presence (p.28), later expressing outright admiration for his tenacity (p.38). He is so won over by von Ebrennac's human qualities that he wants to reply to him (p.29), but he declines to look him in the eye (p.32). He shows sympathy at his halting reading from *Macbeth* (p.42), and expresses at length the extent to which he and his niece missed the familiar presence (p.47). His silence about the chance encounter with von Ebrennac precipitates a scene of increasing tension, followed by a spasm of anger and self-doubt (p.48), a doubt echoed in the phrase 'l'incertitude des désirs contraires' (p.50). In the final scene the respect shown by the uncle's use of 'monsieur', the compassion expressed in 'pathétique' and 'pathétiquement' and the numerous descriptions of von Ebrennac's torment betrayed through his body all combine to convey the uncle's commiseration with the officer's suffering, followed by disappointment as it becomes clear that von Ebrennac will continue to obey a régime which he now fully understands to be evil. The ending is poignant; the uncle notes the last smile of goodbye, then in the final paragraph adopts a tone of blank neutrality, reflecting emptiness after such strong emotion.

Time and suspense

Vercors very skilfully exploits the constraints of the novella by his expert management of time. For example, as the main narrator, it is natural for the uncle to select those aspects which made an impression on him as he looks back over the period of the officer's stay. Although von Ebrennac's arrival in the evening is followed by a description of what happened 'le lendemain matin' (p.24), the next specific occasion mentioned is simply 'un soir', when 'les choses changèrent brusquement' (p.26), the suddenness of the change being in itself a skilful manipulation of the reader's interest. 'Un soir' (again, p.35), 'un jour' (p.47) and 'une fois' (p.31) are deliberately vague, as befits someone reminiscing. They are contrasted with the pinpointing in time of the last visit of the officer: 'Ce fut trois jours plus tard que...' (p.48). The importance of that visit is emphasised simply through repeating 'ce soir' (p.50), while the use of the pluperfect and 'le lendemain' in the very last paragraph convey a bleak finality.

The way in which Vercors makes the officer part of the daily routine of the uncle and niece is by suggesting that his behaviour began to follow a pattern, underlined by his habitual 'je vous souhaite une bonne nuit'. Habit is also conveyed by recapitulating what the uncle and niece had become accustomed to: 'Pendant longtemps — plus d'un mois, — la même scène se répéta chaque jour' (p.25), 'il ne venait pas absolument chaque soir' (p.30), '...plus de cent soirées d'hiver' (p.38). In all these cases, we have a lull in the ongoing events in the story as the uncle sums up what has been happening in between, rounding our picture of the officer, giving us the benefit of his own reflections and anxieties, commenting on the niece's reactions. These pauses, as it were, add greatly to our perception of the characters and their relationships out of all proportion to the short space devoted to them, another example of Vercors's exploitation of the medium of the novella.

Calendar time is slipped naturally into the narrative. Vercors does not, for instance, state baldly that the officer arrived in November, but suggests it: 'ce novembre-là ne fut pas très froid' (p.21); in a similar way, the mention of 'plus de cent soirées d'hiver' makes it credible that spring has come round (p.42). The sound of von Ebrennac's limping footsteps on the stairs before his final appearance serves to connect us with the beginning of the story, as the uncle is reminded of the occasion when he first heard those distinctive steps 'six mois plus tôt (p.49), Vercors thus subtly hinting at a cycle of time being completed. Von Ebrennac's repetition of this 'six mois' (p.52) enhances this and emphasises how often he has talked within that room of his aspirations and feelings, implying thereby the consequent depth of his disillusionment.

Closely allied to this manipulation of time is Vercors's use of suspense as a means of controlling the reader's identification with character and plot, and, as Margaret Atack points out, it is one of the most effective techniques (*44*, pp.64–65). The throwaway use of the pronoun 'Il' as the very first word of the story creates suspense, our curiosity about the identity of its subject remaining unsatisfied until the third page. Indeed, the first two pages of 'overture', with comings and goings which have no great relevance to the plot, could be viewed principally as an exercise in tantalisation, drawn out at the beginning of the second chapter with the use of the unattached pronoun, 'on', and the additional suspense created by the melo-dramatic silhouette at the door. Vercors succeeds in intriguing the reader, who is already asking questions and interacting with the author, ready to respond to the 'messages' in the text. The niece's silence and the uncle sipping his coffee reinforce the tension, which is finally broken when the unknown visitor is revealed as a German officer. After his words of introduction, however, the tense atmosphere builds up again as the silence of the uncle and niece has the effect of disorientating von Ebrennac; the uncle's 'Dieu merci, il a l'air convenable' (p.23) partially dispels the ambiguity, but is countered by the shrug of the niece, which promises further tension.

Once a habitual pattern of visits by the officer has been established, his failure to appear arouses the uncle's curiosity (p.26); when he does arrive, once again there are pauses; this time, his monologue is interspersed with pauses for description in which he changes position or picks up fallen embers from the fire. In these pauses Vercors has created the opportunity for us to engage our interest in him more strongly by following his actions in our mind's eye. The pause after 'A cause de mon père', with the suspense broken by the repetition, followed by the pause after the mention of Briand (pp.27–28) serve to emphasise the expression of his feeling for France which follows, the starting point of which is his father and his father's regard for Briand. The episode from pages 35 to 37 shows a similar use of effective pauses to create suspense, beginning with the misapprehension about who is playing the harmonium (p.35), followed by reflections on the ethereal nature of German music and von Ebrennac's desire to write music on a more human scale (p.36).

Having allowed us to reflect on this idea, he then moves on in an apparently natural way to claim the need for union with France as the only way of achieving his goal. The suspense created by the pauses in this part of the episode allows us to appreciate the ambiguity of this reference to union, particularly given the intimacy of the symbolically offered breast. The thinly veiled sexual connotation is confirmed as he turns to look at the niece immediately afterwards with the phrase 'les obstacles seront surmontés' (p.37). The romantic theme is pursued in the next visits (pp.38–41) when we see the suppressed agitation of the niece on the officer's mention of his fiancée, demonstrated by her breaking the thread of her sewing and her difficulty in re-threading the needle (p.40). A further hint of desired intimacy is added with the reference to her neck on which the officer's gaze rests (p.41).

The intermingled themes of von Ebrennac's love for France and his pursuit of the niece are thus firmly established, and his penultimate visit ends on a note of optimism as he prepares to visit Paris for what he expects to be the greatest day of his life, pending that other 'great day', whose name he has no need to identify (p.44). The reading from *Macbeth*, however, with its prophecy of tragic downfall, strikes the first note of foreboding. With unconscious irony, von Ebrennac ignores the quotation's obvious suitability to Hitler, applying it instead to Darlan. It is also open to interpretation as an indication of his naïvety and as a portent of his own disillusionment and the further tragedy which is to befall France.

Before and during von Ebrennac's last visit the atmosphere of tension and uncertainty is intensified, heightening the reader's curiosity and focusing our attention with an abundance of details of almost cinematic clarity. The suspense produced by the pause in narration is augmented by the invisible presence in the house of von Ebrennac, his pacing upstairs unsettling both uncle and niece. The sense of foreboding ('Cette absence ne me laissait pas l'esprit en repos. Je pensais à lui, je ne sais pas à quel point je n'éprouvais pas du regret, de l'inquiétude', p.47) is further increased when the uncle catches sight of his 'visage [...] pâle et tiré' on their chance encounter at the Kommandantur (p.48). The fact that he tries unsuccessfully to keep this encounter from his niece only emphasises the feelings of disquiet which it produced (p.48). The suspense, broken momentarily by the sound of the familiar approaching footsteps, is drawn out more and more, because the progress of the officer's ever slower steps is interrupted by pauses for reflection, the uncle imagining von Ebrennac's intentions and describing the niece's anguish. There follows the long silence as von Ebrennac hesitates, the uncle picturing him outside the door with hand poised to knock (p.49). His knock, when it eventually comes, is the signal for tumultuous agitation on the part of the uncle, contrasting with the almost trance-like stillness of the niece, gazing fixedly at the door-knob. This sequence ends with the repeated faint knocking and the capitulation of the uncle in the face of the niece's despair, his two words 'Entrez, monsieur' putting an end at last to the months of silence. Throughout this last meeting Vercors manipulates the reader's feelings by this constant alternation of prolonged suspense and momentary respite, which only leads to renewed tension. He intensifies this technique by engineering the pauses during an important announcement and after particularly distressing moments; he also makes us dwell on harrowing descriptions during the period of suspense. Von Ebrennac pauses, for example, after 'Je dois vous adresser des paroles graves' (p.52), during and after 'il faut [...] il faut l'oublier' (ibid), and this emphasises the seriousness of what he has to say. The account of his conversation with his former friends involves skilful placing of pauses to bring out the full horror of each set of revelations from the Nazi officers, together with von Ebrennac's hand, betraying the emotions concealed by his rigid stance and impassive face (p.51), which declares the power of his emotions through its grey pallor (p.57) together with his rigidly clenched jaw (pp.53–54).

Description

'My task which I am trying to achieve is, by the power of the written word to make you hear, to make you feel — it is, before all, to make you see' (*55*, p.xlii). Like Conrad, Vercors places paramount importance on visual description in *Le Silence de la mer*, ever sensitive, as a professional artist, to the detail of colour, shape, posture and movement. The setting is based on Vercors's own house, described in sufficient detail for him to be certain that if his wife read the story, she would recognise it. (*10*, p.201). The depiction of clothes and bodies is similarly precise; von Ebrennac, for example, is not just 'immense et très mince', but brought vividly to our mind's eye by the extra touch, 'En levant le bras il eût touché les solives', and is further individualised by the careful description of the curious relative position of his head, neck and shoulders (p.22). Once more, Conrad's advice is relevant: the writer 'must strenuously aspire to the plasticity of sculpture, to the colour of painting' (*55*, p.xli). The description of the officer's clothes, their texture, style, exact colour, the way they hang, is detailed and, again, pictorial: 'un chandail de grosse laine écrue moulait le torse mince et musclé' (p.26). Our first

introduction to him is deliberately melodramatic, with cinemato-
graphic overtones: 'Je vis l'immense silhouette, la casquette plate,
l'imperméable jeté sur les épaules comme une cape' (p.21). As our
perception is filtered through the uncle's narration, it is only as he
gradually becomes aware of von Ebrennac's physical details that we
discover them: his limp, for example, which the uncle notes only as
the officer goes upstairs (p.23) or the colour of his eyes, visible only
in daylight (p.24). A particularly effective stratagem to exploit the
constraints of space of the novella is Vercors's selection of aspects
which serve more than one purpose. The relative position of rooms in
the house, of objects in the main room, and the size of the house and
room either serve as a link to other information or are conveyed, as it
were, incidentally, as a corollary to something else which is being
remarked on. We deduce right at the beginning of the story that the
house is quite large, because the uncle shows the Germans 'les
chambres libres' (p.19), and there are outbuildings (ibid). The size is
confirmed later by the fact that the Germans mistook it for the
château (pp.24–25). The large kitchen, we are told, opens on to the
garden (hence the officer's footsteps on the terrace are clearly
audible), and there is a second staircase leading to it (which the
officer unexpectedly descends on his first morning), his curiosity
about his new surroundings providing a natural opportunity for
further description of the house. The uncle's narration, in which von
Ebrennac is both observer and observed, has therefore the effect of
limiting our knowledge to the space where the protagonists interact,
giving an intense effect.

The contents of the room are seen principally through von
Ebrennac's eyes: he warms himself in front of the fire (p.26), looks
round him with pleasure to make the important remark that the room
and the house have a soul (p.31), and in this mood of appreciative
reflection proceeds to examine the bookshelves, whose contents
come to embody the threatened culture of France. Our perception of
these objects and their associations is reinforced by subtly recurring
references. The symbolically charged theme of fire, for example, is
introduced by the observation that the uncle had saved logs for a
good fire in the cold weather (p.26); there follow references to the

fire as a source of warmth (pp.26. 30, 36), to falling embers (p.28), the hearth (p.28) and the mantelpiece on which the officer leans (pp.27, 36). Features of the room which von Ebrennac had noticed during his six months take on a new meaning during his final visit: the angel above the window at which he glances on his arrival (p.23) has become an ecstatic celestial being against which the hopelessness of his despair is measured (p.58); the books which he caressed as he spoke of the wished-for union between the two countries symbolise poignantly the culture to be destroyed once the dream of union has been shattered (p.55).

Perhaps because Vercors sees with the eyes of an artist, his descriptions of movement, posture and stillness are remarkably vivid. With the uncle we watch von Ebrennac's every move, pause and action, noting his courteous bow to the niece and his deeper more reverential bow to the uncle, this courtesy being continued with a routine slight bow practically every time he leaves them for the night. Often he makes a movement with his head to emphasise his meaning (three times, for example, on p.32). As if in embarrassment at mentioning an intimate topic, when he speaks of his vocation he turns his back to them (p.36); when he turns to face to them again the effect is to lay added emphasis on the faintly threatening words 'Les obstacles seront surmontés' (p.37). We follow him as he moves around the room and as he pauses, often in moments of suspense, when there is almost the effect of a tableau, usually broken by some movement. This technique allows us to observe him very closely, for instance, as he warms himself in front of the fire, altering his position several times (pp.26–29) and, most strikingly, in his rigid stance throughout his last visit, broken by the movements of his face and hand (pp.51–58). He is often framed in the doorway to symbolise the fact that he does not belong (pp.21, 24, 25, 26, 41, 51, 57, 59), the first and last references framing the story in a pleasing symmetry. The niece's erect posture (pp.21, 22. 23) alters dramatically to illustrate the intolerable strain she is under as von Ebrennac pauses outside the door (p.49), and when her uncle ventures to say that the officer seems all right, her shrug speaks volumes (p.23). Vercors finds plausible ways of allowing the uncle to describe in asides the

niece's posture and his own, their immobility, for example, after the
officer arrives (p.22) or their customary positions during the evening
visits, he seated in his deep armchair (pp.27, 51) and his niece at her
work. In fact, although the niece's hands are usually busy and the
uncle sits and smokes, the overall impression conveyed is one of
fascinated stillness, contrast-ing with the officer talking, standing,
crouching, or walking round the room, making him the cynosure of
our eyes as well as of theirs.

Colour plays an important part in helping us visualise
characters and settings, and is sometimes very precisely defined in
exact shades; for example one of von Ebrennac's jackets is 'de tweed
bleu acier enchevêtré de mailles d'un brun chaud' (p.26) , while
another is 'en jersey de laine couleur de bure' (p.42). Where the
colours are not described in detail, it is because the material is
associated with a certain shade, like 'flanelle grise' (p.26), 'carreaux
rouges' (p.21) and 'vieilles tuiles brunes' (p.24). Light and dark are
both used for symbolic purposes, as we shall see later, and for visual
contrast; the niece, in particular, is described in terms of this contrast,
neatly encapsulated in the evocative phrase 'la nuque frêle et pâle
d'où les cheveux s'élevaient en torsades de sombre acajou' (p.41).
Like her skin, her eyes are pale (pp.52, 59); so are those of von
Ebrennac, but his hair is a Teutonic blond (p.22). Pallor is described
with considerable exactitude when reflecting emotional strain: the
niece is 'd'une pâleur lunaire' (p.58) as she anticipates the entrance
of von Ebrennac, whose own pallor is minutely depicted (p.57). Light
and shade also play a part in our visualisation of the room; for
example, our first unforgettable sight of the officer occurs at night,
with the uncle 'relativement dans l'ombre' (p.21), and later von
Ebrennac comments appreciatively on the firelight (p.31).

Not surprisingly, in a story in which two of the three protagonists are mute, there is much use of body language as a means of
betraying thoughts and feelings; like Conrad, it is through the eyes,
hands and faces of his characters that Vercors reveals the inner
drama. These bodily signs, of course, are seen through the eyes of the
uncle, who reminds us from time to time of his status as literal viewer
of the action, for instance in his contemplation of von Ebrennac at

the harmonium: 'je *considérai* le long buste devant l'instrument'(p.35) or in describing the expression of his niece: 'je *voyais* bien (p.47) and particularly throughout the final scene: 'je *vis* les paupières' (p.49); 'je *regardai* ma nièce' (p.50); 'je *voyais* saillir les pommettes' (p.54); 'je le *regardais*', 'je *regardais*'. 'je *vis*' (p.57) (my emphases). At these moments we too become aware of our own position as onlookers and our attention is consequently sharpened: as von Ebrennac approaches, an aspect of the mounting tension is that we see the uncle as a horrified observer, watching in self-imposed silence as his niece's face takes on the appearance of a tragic mask and the beads of sweat burst out on her brow (p.59).

There are a number of direct references to eyes in the story. The uncle cannot, of course, describe his own eyes, but he does say that he refuses to enter into eye contact with von Ebrennac (p.32) as an indication of unwillingness to enter into a relationship. Von Ebrennac's gaze is directed almost exclusively at the niece, with remarkable frequency and insistence. His lingering, almost intrusive contemplation of her is noted on their first meeting: 'Il détourna *enfin* les yeux' (p.23) and regularly thereafter: 'Ses yeux *s'attardaient* sur le profil incliné de ma nièce' (p.35); 'il regardait ma nièce [...] *avec une insistence grave*' (p.33) (my emphases). The niece's eyes, normally averted, are expressive of proud indignation when the uncle suggests they break their silence (p.29); later, in a striking repeated comparison, her stare is compared to that of an eagle-owl (pp.49 and 50). The most significant mention of her eyes, however, is when she at last acknowledges her feelings for von Ebrennac by looking at him for the first time, provoking the literal and symbolic description of her eyes: 'Oh welch' ein Licht!' (p.52), emphasised by von Ebrennac's gesture of warding off the light with his hand. Hitherto her refusal of him has been evident not only in her rigid posture and her silence, but also in her determination not to look at him, either pretending he is not there (pp.21, 22), affecting to be absorbed in her work (pp.27, 41) or showing her profile (pp.32, 33). Now, in his apparently desperate situation, by looking him full in the face she offers him a ray of hope. Her eyes are 'pâles et dilatés' when von Ebrennac fixes his gaze on them (p.54); this gaze, in which they remain locked 'comme [...] la barque à l'anneau de la rive', is the most moving feature of his slow departure. The emphasis on the duration and the intensity of their looking at each other is also the most important ingredient in the suspense created at this point, the niece's forming her lips for 'Adieu' anticipated by 'les yeux de Werner brillèrent (p.59), the sudden use of his Christian name symbolising the necessarily tacit intimacy of the relationship. Von Ebrennac's eyes have already been evoked in this scene in two bird images: first, that of a falcon, as he darts a sudden anguished glance at the uncle with wide-open eyes (p.51, p.57), and then that of a lost night-flying bird (p.55), which vividly conveys his disorientation as he looks wildly round the comfortable room where he had once expounded his now sadly incongruous idealistic philosophy.

Hands betray the emotions no less than eyes, as the uncle notes 'j'appris ce jour-là qu'une main peut, pour qui sait l'observer, refléter les émotions aussi bien qu'un visage' (p.51), and we have seen the importance of the niece's hands in her progressive loss of coordination as she struggles with her feelings, a decline manifested in the 'léger tremblement des doigts' registered by the uncle (p.38). Her hands fall into her lap to express weariness (p.48) and submission when they lie 'penchées et inertes comme des barques échouées sur le sable' (p.52). Hands also feature in Jean Cocteau's design on her shawl, whose disturbing pattern could be seen as an analogue of her own inner agitation (p.49), while naming this well-known contemporary figure again brings the story and its warning very firmly into the real world. The uncle's hands are involved only in the gestures of lighting and smoking his pipe (pp.23, 27, 29, 48), which would seem to give an air of relaxed domesticity were it not for tension noted at various times on the part of both uncle and niece. Von Ebrennac has the sensitive hands of a musician: '...les mains longues, fines, nerveuses, dont les doigts se déplaçaient sur les touches commes des individus autonomes' (p.35). His gestures frequently declare his mood or his state of mind, whether hesitant: his enigmatic gesture on arrival (p.23), relaxed: 'les mains dans les poches de sa veste' (p.27), brisk and cheerful: tapping his jacket pocket (p.43), or defeated: 'il leva légèrement une main, que presque aussitôt il laissa retomber' (p.48). In the final scene it is the uncontrollable workings of his hand which reveal his inner torment as it stretches and clenches (p.51) and then performs an extraordinary dancing movement in front of his face before he clutches his forehead (p.57), and finally, in exhaustion, lets his hands fall (p.58).

Von Ebrennac's characteristic expression is a smile, 'cette expression d'approbation à la fois souriante et grave qui avait été la sienne dès le premier jour' (p.38), and which accompanies his contemplation of the room, its books and, most importantly, the niece. This amiability, which Vercors is at pains to emphasise — there are fourteen references to his smile between pages 21 and 43 — is of course the very aspect for which he was taken to task by those who misunderstood the message of the story (see CODA, Reactions to *Le Silence de la mer*.) It is all the more dangerously attractive for not being simply the expression of a generalised affability but a nuanced and occasionally hesitant or self-deprecating manifestation of von Ebrennac's moods, particularly in the face of the silent defiance of the niece, 'immanquablement sévère et insensible' (p.25). In the war of wills between the officer and niece, the 'sorte d'approbation souriante' (p.26) with which he counters her stubbornness is perhaps one of his most subversive weapons. Touchingly, after the agonising contortion of his features during the last scene, we are left with the final image of him after he has received the blessing of the niece's 'Adieu' (p.59), closing the circle which begins with the discreet smile with which he greets his hosts on his arrival (p.21).

The grotesque deformations of his face in the final encounter are particularly shocking by contrast with the picture we have built up of the handsome, quietly smiling musician: at first a rigidity which renders him almost unrecognisable (p.51), then a clenching of the jaw, bulging veins and a sudden spasm (pp.53–54), leaving his face the colour of mottled grey plaster (p.57). The niece's appearance is similarly transformed from one of obdurate impassivity, head bowed over her work, to a tragic, staring intensity. However, in her case the change is the revelation, the 'drame intime soudain dévoilé' (p.50) of a process which has been pursuing its course throughout the story,

hitherto revealed, as we have seen, by a series of carefully placed
hints and clues. When von Ebrennac returns from Paris, his brooding
and invisible presence in the house shows on the niece's face in the
'quelques lignes légères qui marquaient son visage d'une expression
à la fois butée et attentive', and again, the sound of his pacing
overhead is reflected in the 'application têtue' with which she
suddenly applies herself to her sewing (p.47). This complex web of
suppressed emotions, in which love, guilt, duty and pride are
mingled, finds its catharsis at the moment she raises her eyes to meet
those of the officer.

Visual description is taken a stage further by Vercors's
suggestive use of simile and metaphor. Strong visual description
precedes 'comme', 'comme si' or 'comme pour', which are
frequently used to provide a stimulus for the imagination. The niece
passes her hand over her forehead 'comme pour chasser une
migraine' (p.48), a gesture we can instantly picture and, what is
more, the state of mind it represents. Sometimes these expressions
are used to extend a description or add an extra dimension: the
suspense created by von Ebrennac's non-appearance after his visit to
Paris is emphasised by his shaking his head in the Kommandantur
'comme s'il se fût dit: non, à lui-même' (ibid), adding to the mood of
foreboding. An evocative simile finally breaks the long suspense of
his last visit: '…et son visage et tout son corps semblèrent s'assoupir
comme après un bain reposant' (p.59). Two of the most powerful
similes in the story are used together to intensify the impression on
the reader of von Ebrennac's anguished state of mind: the clenching
of his jaw is followed by a facial spasm 'dans une sorte de
frémissement souterrain, comme fait un coup de brise sur un lac;
comme, aux premières bulles, la pellicule de crême durcie à la
surface d'un lait qu'on fait bouillir' (p.54). Like all Vercors's similes
and metaphors, these two comparisons are taken from everyday life,
but the combination of their differing associations — the elemental
forces of nature in the one as opposed to the familiar domesticity of
the other — work on the imagination in a way that is anything but
banal. A few pages later von Ebrennac's pallor is evoked in
extremely precise terms: 'pâle, — non pas comme de la cire, mais

comme le plâtre de certains murs délabrés: gris avec des taches plus blanches de salpêtre' (p.57). This is a fine example of Vercors's economy of expression, in which in a very short space four strong visual images fuse to compose an accurate description, its verisimilitude reinforced by the rejection of the conventional association of pallor with a 'waxy' appearance.

One of the principal metaphorical associations throughout the story is that of the union of France and Germany seen as a marriage, of which the tale of Beauty and the Beast provides a symbolic illustration. Parallel to and inextricably linked with the abstract notion of France, with her civilisation and culture, as a healing and succouring ally of Germany, runs the real life theme of von Ebrennac's love of the niece. The intermingling of the two themes is achieved by the frequent personification of France elsewhere as 'Marianne', and by the book-lined room as a microcosm of France and her culture, though in neither case in the text is there a crude equation, but associations of ideas which the reader can exploit. The ambiguity of the language used ('amour', 'union', 'mariage') facilitates the slide from one level of meaning to another. This process begins with von Ebrennac's first words on the subject, in which France is personified as 'la Princesse Lointaine', (p.27, and see 82, pp.123–35) and continues some lines later with 'unir, comme mari et femme' (p.28). The monologues which follow build on this association of ideas (including the highly-charged image of France offering her breast (p.36), mentioned above), to the point where von Ebrennac looks forward to being welcomed as a son of a French village like the one where he is now (p. 37), which can be seen as a veiled proposal of marriage.

The necessity of France to become the 'healer' of Germany's soul is illustrated by the story of von Ebrennac's fiancée, who pulls the legs off a mosquito, and its conclusion: 'Ainsi sont aussi chez nous les hommes politiques' (p.40). Having shown this amount of perspicacity, von Ebrennac nevertheless reveals the naïvety that led to charges of collaborationism, believing that by the enlightening civilisation of France, the worst of Nazis can be purified. As the Intellectual Resistance realised, the Nazis were engaged in ideological warfare and Vercors shows that because they are only too aware of the power of France's soul, they seek to annihilate it. The real depths of German perfidy are revealed on pages 53–54, where the mirror image of von Ebrennac's idealism is presented: whereas he wished to drink nourishing milk from the breast of France, his colleagues wish to purge Europe of her poison; whereas he believed that 'la France les [les Allemands] guérira' (p.41), they reverse this to 'nous guérirons l'Europe de cette peste [la France]!' (p.54).

The weather and light are also features of the story which have symbolic value. The weather is unseasonal and, like the times, out of joint; autumn is mild (ce novembre-là ne fut pas très froid', p.21) but July is cold (p.49) and the story ends on a symbolic note of desolation and foreboding, the words 'il me sembla' enhancing the symbolic effect. Light is used for its traditionally positive associations, for example when the officer compares the fire and the quality of light it bestows with that in his own house (p.31). Significantly, it is linked here with his perusal of a bookcase, a blending of the notions of literal and metaphorical illumination which is echoed in the final scene by the 'reliures doucement luisant dans la pénombre' (p.55), the semi-darkness suggestive of the shadows threatening French culture. The notion of darkness as symbolic of death, both literal and spiritual, is evident in the quotation from *Othello* which divides the two parts of the story and which inspired the title of the English translation by Cyril Connolly, *Put Out the Light*. The desperation shown in: 'Ils éteindront la flamme tout à fait! cria-t-il. L'Europe ne sera plus éclairée par cette lumière!' (p.55), reminds us of Vercors's heightened consciousness of French literature as a flame of cultural heritage to show the Nazis and the rest of the world 'la preuve de la survivance [...] de la vie spirituelle française. La preuve qu'elle tenait allumé dans la nuit, comme les moines de jadis, le flambeau dont la flamme se transmettait de main en main et même, s'il le fallait, de génération en génération pour enfin, au bout du tunnel, reparaître vivante au grand jour' (*10*), p.189)

Sounds and Voice

The story begins with two sounds — knocking and the noise of
footsteps — which are used by Vercors at various points throughout
the *récit* both to indicate the invisible presence of the officer and as a
technique of creating suspense. The sound of boot-heels (p.21) is
initially ominous, as they would inevitably have recalled the sound of
Nazi jackboots, and, as Margaret Atack points out, his footsteps and
slight accent, together with his entourage's preparations and attempts
at French set them apart as the enemy (*44*, p.78). The threat is
defused, however, by von Ebrennac's amiable demeanour and the
significant detail of his lameness, which has the effect of making him
appear vulnerable and also gives a characteristic and compelling
distinctiveness to his footfall. The sound of his slow and uneven
progress through the house adds a note of anticipation to the surprise
of his first appearance in civilian clothes (p.26), and after his return
from Paris his footsteps above work on the nerves of both uncle and
niece (p.47). His final appearance is prefaced by a masterly passage
of writing charged with suspense as the officer's slow but implacable
descent makes the stairs 'gémir' and 'crier', words themselves
denoting painful sounds, the tension thus created reducing the niece
to the point of collapse. His knock at this point is also described in
precise detail ('trois coups pleins et lents, les coups assurés et calmes
d'une décision sans retour', p.49), which recalls the traditional
curtain-raising knocks in French theatres, appropriately heralding a
highly charged dramatic scene. These knocks are in marked contrast
to von Ebrennac's previous perfunctory taps which were merely the
manifestation of his natural politeness, the officer always opening the
door himself without waiting for the reply that he knows will not be
forthcoming. Now, for the first time, he waits outside, as if to force
their submission. When it seems clear that there will be no reply, he
touchingly gives two further hesitant knocks, by which we can guess
his despairing state of mind.

His voice, though not specifically melodious, has a certain
hypnotic quality which is conveyed by the repeated use of the
adjectives 'bourdonnant' and 'sourd' along with other epithets
expressive of a measured and gentle musicality ('léger', 'chantant',

'doucement', 'lente'). This comforting inflection is ideally suited to the atmosphere of story-telling which pervades the first part of the narrative, the words seeming not to break the silence but somehow to be born out of it (p.27). Lulled and fascinated, the uncle is forced at length to express his admiration for von Ebrennac: 'jamais il ne fut tenté de secouer cet implacable silence par quelque violence de langage' (p.38). Vercors's aim, of course, is to manipulate the mood of contemporary readers of this *œuvre de circonstance*, drawing them into this enclosed, separate world. Through the constant repetition of von Ebrennac's tone of voice Vercors has ensured that they become familiar with its 'bourdonne-ment sourd et chantant', so that when he expresses his anguish in the final scene, they are taken aback by the violent changes in his speech, and so listen all the more closely to his spine-chilling revelations. The effort it takes him to begin his appalling revelation is conveyed by the popping noise of his tense lips 'comme le goulot débouché d'une bouteille vide', followed by his gasping 'avec un effort d'asthmatique' (p.52). Barely audible tones, like 'Oh welch' ein Licht!' (p.52) and the subtle exploitation of the established tone: 'sa voix était plus sourde que jamais' (p.52) and 'sourde, sourde, sourde' (p.53) are part of a whole range of vocal expression and volume which powerfully express the significance of each utterance. In contrast to the softer and softer repetitions of 'pas d'espoir' comes the sudden shout like a bugle call when he says it for the last time (p.54). His grief at the impending fate of French culture gives way to a desperate cry, then to 'Nevermore!', chillingly described: 'Et sa voix creuse et grave fit vibrer jusqu'au creux de ma poitrine, inattendu et saisissant, le cri dont l'ultime syllabe traînait comme une frémissante plainte' (p.55), the reference to Poe's poem *The Raven* adding a note of nightmare and terror. After this profoundly affecting scene the familiar departing words 'je vous souhaite une bonne nuit', spoken in a voice 'étrangement déuée d'expression' are particularly poignant in contrast to the friendly optimism of his earlier visits (p.59).

The uncle and niece say only three words between them to von Ebrennac throughout the story, the uncle's 'Entrez, monsieur' with which the final scene opens and the niece's barely audible 'Adieu' with which it closes, both utterances in response to the emotional situation of the moment, the uncle no longer able to bear the agony of his niece and the niece moved to pity by the departure of von Ebrennac.

Silence

The uncle, and in particular the niece, would in their silent determination serve as an antidote to the self-interest that so many French people had demonstrated in the immediate aftermath of the invasion and which had so disgusted Vercors. At the same time, however, many would identify with the uncle's hesitations over maintaining the silence while considering the niece's attitude too extreme. It is only at the end of the narrative that Vercors allows von Ebrennac's revelations to demonstrate that even the most appealing servant of Hitler must be resisted by uncompromising silence, both literally and also metaphorically, in terms of absolute non-collaboration.

As the story unfolds, it becomes obvious that, paradoxically, through choosing to wield their weapon of silence, both uncle and niece are making a painful sacrifice, while it is ineffectual against its intended target, von Ebrennac, who, in fact, positively seems to revel in it, having expressed his initial admiration at the patriotism it represents (p.23). He returns most evenings to pursue his monologue, the uncle noting, perhaps a touch wryly, that 'il semblait bien être celui de nous trois qui s'y trouvait le plus à l'aise' (p.38). Furthermore, although the uncle and niece are determined to pursue their lives as normal, their commitment to silence in the officer's presence means that they cannot speak to each other while he is there, creating awkwardness and heightening the niece's suffering and the uncle's indecision over the appropriateness of the silence. Such is the effect of von Ebrennac on them that they are silent even in his absence, when, as we have seen, he is present in their thoughts, charging the atmosphere between them, most poignantly after his departure: 'Elle me servit en silence. Nous bûmes en silence' (p.60).

Von Ebrennac's counter-weapon, used to great effect, is his charm. Although physically dominating, although an occupying enemy officer, although occasionally betraying steely determination, he adopts a deferential humility — abandoning his uniform, knocking before entering, remaining standing — and shows his sensitivity: his musicianship, his love of books, his grave smile. These, added to his striking appearance, his vulnerability and attractive voice, mean that he offers the niece an agonising choice. Into a well-regulated, unexciting existence for a young woman, comes someone who could be the answer to every maiden's prayer, declaring his love and offering marriage in thinly veiled symbolic terms. The example of the niece, therefore, resisting her uncle's occasional urge to compromise and placing patriotism above her own feelings, all the while wrestling with them in self-imposed silence, is one of supreme self-sacrifice.

The silence is described as an almost tangible presence, symbolising a barrier between the officer and his hosts, and between the uncle and niece. It marks their patriotic protest (*44*, p.67) and, quoting Bossuet, Guéhenno calls the adoption of this stance 'le silence du zèle' (*65*, p.39). Von Ebrennac seems to measure it (p.21), it is heavy (p.27), it is like a gas which can be inhaled, permeating the room (p.38), it resembles thick fog, and becomes leaden when combined with the motionless postures of uncle and niece (p.22). These postures perhaps symbolise the awkwardness between them, because they cannot bring themselves to ignore the officer and chat as normal. Instead they try, sometimes unsuccessfully (p.35), to read each other's expression. Within this atmosphere the sounds in the story, footsteps, knocks, tones of voice, all impinge on the ear and acquire a greater significance, resonating as they do in isolation. Von Ebrennac's reaction to his hosts' indifference is to respect them all the more for it (pp.32–33); in fact, the niece's silence, far from quelling his ardour, actually inflames his passion, increasing his determination to win her over: 'Mon intention était que ce fût son silence même qui enflammât von Ebrennac, déjà amant de la France, au point de les confondre dans son esprit' (*86*). Through expert exploitation of the emotions and through the choice of a story medium, the inevitable equation of patriotism with non-collaboration and in turn with painful self-sacrifice impinges powerfully on the consciousness of Vercors's intended readers. The height of the niece's silent agony coincides with the move from story to reality, facing every contemporary French reader with the question 'Mais où est MON devoir?' (p.58).

The Sea

Vercors's long-standing fascination with the sea meant that sea imagery came very naturally to him, and it appears in several of his works. Here, he uses it to illustrate and recommend a dignified silence which masks terrible struggles, contradictions, deep feelings and conflicting desires, which the uncle and niece hide under the regular pattern of their daily routine and their carefully schooled expressions. He was an experienced sailor of yachts he built himself (*10*, p.50), and had long been fascinated by the paradox of the smooth surface of the sea concealing violence in its depths, as he told Gilles Plazy:

—*Pourquoi ce titre*: *Le Silence de la mer*?

—C'est une image qui m'a toujours poursuivie: la mer, 'toit tranquille' comme l'appelle Valéry, si calme et silencieuse sous le ciel bleu, n'en dissimule pas moins la mêlée des bêtes dans les profondeurs, qui s'entre-déchirent, s'entre-dévorent. Ainsi, sous le silence de la jeune fille et de son oncle, se trouve toute l'ardeur des sentiments cachés, toute la violence d'un combat spirituel. (*13*, p.33)

Because of Oudeville's comment that the meaning of the title was insufficiently clear, Vercors added the following simile :'—comme, sous la calme surface des eaux, la mêlée des bêtes dans la mer, —je sentais grouiller la vie sous-marine des sentiments cachés, des désirs et des pensées qui se nient et se luttent' (p.55). Besides explaining the rationale of the uncle's and niece's behaviour, this image also reflects the situation of Vercors himself, eschewing propaganda to communicate his own inner turmoil through the controlled medium of a story, and exercising the necessary self-discipline to maintain the

secret of his true identity. By contrast, von Ebrennac's candid smile,
his readiness to talk about himself, his thoughts and feelings, show
the confidence of the benevolent conqueror. It is significant that
when he has been disabused, he becomes relatively inarticulate and
only his hand betrays his feelings; his face and eyes, like the surface
of the sea, remain impassive. There is further irony in his confident
diagnosis of the problem facing Europe, as he explains that the Nazis
know that they could become 'vraiment grands et purs' on contact
with France's healing powers (p.41). In fact, he had not realised just
what the 'vie sous-marine' of the Nazis was like.

It is the 'vie sous-marine' of the *récit,* which we as readers
must interpret from the clues on the surface, that is, through the
uncle's narration, which is one of the elements of its continuing
fascination. We scrutinise the tacit messages of the uncle and niece,
which have as their origin the feelings they are unable to express
openly, to the extent that even in von Ebrennac's absence, the niece's
feelings show only in her facial expression (p.29). Just as we are
aware of these signs of her 'vie sous-marine', so we join with the
uncle in his uncertainty and his use of 'comme', 'comme si' and
'comme pour' in trying to weigh up the full significance of words and
gestures. When von Ebrennac does not appear after his visit to Paris,
his presence is detected from the clues he cannot help leaving (p.47).
The niece shows 'une divination de félin' as she seems to be able to
interpret the truth her uncle is trying to hide (p.48). Her sufferings are
finally 'soudain dévoilé' not by words, but by her expression (p.50).

A number of other images and expressions reinforce the
maritime associations of the title: the uncle looks at the niece 'pour
pécher dans ses yeux un encouragement ou un signe' (p.50); the
niece's hands, in useless rest, are like 'des barques échouées sur le
sable' (p.52), and von Ebrennac's forehead is like 'un grelin
d'amarre' (p.54). However, it is during his long-drawn out leave-
taking that such vocabulary powerfully symbolises the strength of the
feelings between himself and the niece: 'Ses pupilles, celles de la
jeune fille, amarrées comme dans le courant, la barque à l'anneau de
la rive, semblaient l'être par un fil si tendu, si raide, qu'on n'eût pas
osé passer un doigt entre leurs yeux' (p.59).

Like one of the mysteries of the sea, von Ebrennac's departure has been silent and secret, contrasted with the 'grand déploiement d'appareil militaire' (p.19) which heralded his arrival. The final melancholy scene of the silent, pensive breakfast reflects not only the mood of the uncle and niece, but that of French readers of the time faced with von Ebrennac's dire warning. Like the actual situation of the Occupation, the *récit* is unfinished and no loose ends are tied up, underlining the change from a story to a reflection of contemporary reality. Physically, now, too, a shift takes place to a glimpse of the world outside, accentuating the inevitable necessity of continuing to live under the Occupation: 'Dehors luisait au travers de la brume un pâle soleil' (p.60). Vercors offers the 'pâle soleil' visible though the mist of uncertainty as a slightly optimistic sign on the surface of the sea of turmoil, duplicity and suffering which already characterised the Occupation, and which he foresaw would intensify. Indeed, the final 'Il me sembla qu'il faisait très froid' (p.60) indicates that any optimism is very guarded, the stark finality of the syntax echoing the literal and metaphorical chill of the meaning.

Select Bibliography

All French items are published in Paris unless otherwise indicated.

EDITIONS OF LE SILENCE DE LA MER

1. Editions de Minuit, 1942.
2. London, Les Cahiers du Silence, 1943 (Preface by Maurice Druon).
3. London, Macmillan, 1944 (Introduction by A. Mark).
4. *Put Out the Light*, translation by Cyril Connolly (London, Macmillan, 1944).
5. *Le Silence de la mer et autres récits* (Albin Michel, 1951, Livre de Poche, 1959, 1993) All page references are to this last edition.
6. Stokes, L. and Brown, J. *Silence of the Sea/Le Silence de la mer* (NewYork, Oxford, Berg, 1991).
7. Play version (Actes Sud-Papiers, 1990).
8. Film version by Jean-Pierre Melville, 1948.

VERCORS'S LIFE

9. Vercors, *PPC (Pour Prendre Congé)* (Albin Michel, 1957).
10. Vercors, *La Bataille du silence* (Vercors et Presses de la Cité, 1967, Editions de Minuit, 1992).
11. Konstantinovic, R.D., *Vercors, écrivain et dessinateur* (Klincksieck, 1969).
12. *Vercors, écrivain né de la nuit* (Bibliothèque du Travail, 2, No 125, 1981).
13. *A dire vrai (Entretiens de Vercors avec Gilles Plazy)* (François Bourin, 1991).

OBITUARIES AND TRIBUTES

14. Plazy, G., *Le Monde*, 13 June 1991.
15. Druon, M., *Le Figaro*, 12 June 1991.
16. Hommage à Vercors et à Jacques Lecompte-Boinet, Passerelle des Arts, Paris, 25 February, 1992 (Secrétariat d'Etat aux anciens combattants).

INTERVIEWS AND REVIEWS

17. Boyer de Latour, P., 'Vercors: "Je ne suis pas l'homme d'un seul livre" ', *Le Figaro littéraire*, 2 April 1991.
18. Daix, P., 'Vercors et le fantastique' (interview with Vercors about *Sylva) Les Lettres françaises*, 6 April 1961.
19. Malffrand, T., 'L'Invité du mois: Vercors', *Notre 6e*, 29 May 1990, p.13.
20. Plazy, G.: 'L'Etoile de minuit', *Le Monde*, 20 March 1992.

SELECTED ALBUMS AND ILLUSTRATIONS BY JEAN BRULLER

21. Recettes pratiques de mort violente (Petit manuel du parfait suicide) (Vercors, 19 rue Servandoni, 1926).
22. Nouvelle clé des songes (Creuzevault, 1934).
23. Silences (Villiers-sur-Morin, Vercors, 1937).
24. La Danse des Vivants, in Relevés trimestriels, preface by Jules Romains (Aux Nourritures terrestres, 1932–1938).
25. Silence, Edgar Allan Poe (Villiers-sur-Morin, Vercors, 1942).
26. Hamlet, Shakespeare, adapted and translated in collaboration with Rita Barisse (Vialetay, 1965).

SELECTED WORKS BY VERCORS

27. *La Marche à l'étoile* (Les Editions de Minuit, 1943).
28. *Le Sable du temps* (Emile Paul 1945).
29. *Les Armes de la nuit* (Les Editions de Minuit, 1946).
30. *Les Mots* (Les Editions de Minuit, 1947).
31. *Les Yeux et la lumière* (Emile Paul, 1948).
32. *Le Songe* and *Ce jour-là* (Poésie 49, 1949).
33. *Plus ou moins homme* (Albin Michel, 1950).
34. *La Puissance du jour* (Albin Michel, 1951).
35. *Les Animaux dénaturé*s (Albin Michel, 1952).
36. *Portrait d'une amitié* (Albin Michel, 1954).
37. *Sylva* (Grasset and Presses Pocket,1961, Grasset, 1992).
38. *Zoo ou l'Assassin philanthrope* (Galilée,1963, 1978).
39. *Les Chemins de l'être* (Albin Michel, 1965).
40. *Ce que je crois* (Grasset, 1975).
41. *Sens et non-sens de l'histoire* (Galilée, 1978).
42. Cent ans d'histoire de France, I: Moi, Aristide Briand (Plon, 1981, Brussels, Editions Complexe, 1993); II: Les Occasions perdues (Plon, 1982); III: Les Nouveaux jours (Plon, 1984).
43. *Anne Boleyn* (Perrin, 1985).

LITERARY CRITICISM

44. Atack, M., Literature and the French Resistance: Cultural Politics and Narrative Forms 1940–1950 (Manchester, Manchester University Press, 1989).

45. Cesbron, G. and Jacquin, G. (eds.) Vercors (Jean Bruller) et son œuvre, Actes du colloque, Université d'Angers, mai 1995 (l'Harmattan, 1999).

46. Cresseaux, J.P., Etude sur Vercors, Le silence de la mer (Coll. Résonances Ellipses Edition Marketing, 1999).

47. Cruickshank, J. (ed.), French Literature and its Background, 6: The Twentieth Century (London, Oxford, New York, Oxford University Press, 1970).

48. Girard, M., Guide illustré de la littérature moderne 1918–49 (Seghers, 1949).

49. Kidd, W., Le Silence de la mer et autres recits, Glasgow Introductory Guides to French Texts (Glasgow, University of Glasgow French and German Publications, 1991).

50. Kidd, W., 'Von Ebrennac, Prince of Denmark?', *French Studies Bulletin,* 22, (Spring 1987), pp.17–19.

51. Koestler, A., 'The French flu' in *The Yogi and the Commissar* (London, Jonathan Cape, 1946, pp.26–27, first published in *The Tribune,* November, 1943, Macmillan, 1946).

52. Leff, A.A., 'Les Editions de Minuit: Purveyors of propaganda' (*The French Review,* vol.74, no.4, March 2001).

53. Sartre, J.-P., *Situations II (Qu'est-ce que la littérature?)* (Gallimard, 1948).

54. Sartre, J.-P., *Situations III* (Gallimard, 1949).

ON CONRAD

55. Conrad, J., Preface to *The Nigger of the Narcissus* (Oxford and New York, Oxford University Press, The World's Classics series, 1984).

56. Leavis, F.R., *The Great Tradition* (London, Chatto and Windus, 1950).

57. Lothe, J., *Conrad's Narrative Method* (Oxford and New York, Oxford University Press, Clarendon series, 1989).

HISTORICAL BACKGROUND

58. Aubrac, L., Ils partiront dans l'ivresse (Lyon, mai 43, Londres, février 44), (Editions du Seuil, 1984).

59. Azéma, J.-P., De Munich à la Libération, 1928–1944 (Editions du Seuil, 1979).

60. Bellanger, C., La Presse clandestine, 1940–44 (Armand Colin, 1945).

61. Bertin, C., Les Femmes sous l'Occupation (Stock, 1993).
62. Cobban, A., A History of Modern France, III (London, Penguin, 1965).
63. Conan, E., 'Enquête sur un crime oublié' (L'Express, 4 mai 1990, pp. 22–31).
64. Dalloz, P., Vérités sur le drame du Vercors (Fernand Lanvres, 1979).
65. Debû-Bridel, J. (ed.), La Résistance intellectuelle: textes et témoignages (Julliard, 1970).
66. Debû-Bridel, J., Les Editions de Minuit: historique et bibliographie (Editions de Minuit, 1945).
67. De Gaulle, C., Mémoires de guerre: L'Appel (Librairie Plon, 1954).
68. Higgins, I. (ed.), Anthology of Second World War French Poetry (London, Methuen, 1982).
69. Jackson, J., France, the Dark Years (O.U.P., 2001).
70. Kedward, R. and Austin, A. Vichy France and the Resistance: Culture and Ideology (London and Sydney, Croom Helm, 1985).
71. Marcou, L., Elsa Triolet, les yeux et la mémoire (Plon, 1994).
72. Michel, H., Histoire de la Résistance (Collection: Que sais-je?, Presses Universitaires de France, 1952).
73. Michel, H., Paris résistant (Albin Michel, 1982).
74. Nettelbeck, C. (ed.), War and Identity: The French and the Second World War, an Anthology of Texts (London, Methuen, 1987).
75. Noguères, H. et al., Histoire de la Résistance en France, 5 vols. (Robert Laffont, 1967 and 1969).
76. Noguères, H., La Vie quotidienne des résistants de l'Armistice à la Libération (1940–1945) (Hachette, 1984).
77. Ophuls, M., Le Chagrin et la pitié (Film, 1969).
78. Proud, J.K., Children and Propaganda — Il était une fois…Fiction and Fairy Tale in Vichy France (Intellect, 1995).
79. Ragache, G. and J.-R. Ragache, La Vie quotidienne des artistes et des écrivains sous l'occupation de 1940–1944 (Hachette 1988).
80. Seghers, P., La Résistance et ses poètes, 2 vols (Hachette, 1974).
81. Simonin, A., Les Editions de Minuit 1942–1955: Le Devoir d'insoumission (IMEC, 1994).
82. Steel, J., Littératures de l'ombre, récits et nouvelles de la Résistance (Presse de la Fondation Nationale des Sciences Politiques, 1991).
83. Veillon, D., La Collaboration (Livre de Poche, 1984).
84. Webster, P., Pétain's crime (Pan, 2001).

LETTERS TO THE AUTHOR FROM VERCORS AND FROM MME
BRULLER-VERCORS QUOTED IN THE TEXT

85. 6 February, 1988.
86. 12 April, 1988.
87. 26 July, 1993.